Disaster Recovery

A Survivor's Guide to Insurance

State of California Edition

ISBN: 978-0-615-53436-7

Library of Congress Number: 2011937940

Disclaimer

Community Assisting Recovery, Inc. (aka CARe, Inc. or CARe) is not a
law firm and does not act as your attorney nor does it interact with your
insurance company on your behalf. This document was prepared for
educational purposes, does not substitute for the advice of an attorney
and should not be construed as legal advice. If you need legal
representation, are involved in litigation, or have complex legal issues
that cannot be handled or dealt with on your own, you should seek
competent legal advice and/or hire an attorney.

Acknowledgements

We'd like to thank the San Diego Foundation for major funding in support of this project, as well as the generous individuals whose donations to CARe funded the balance of the project. We'd also like to extend our appreciation to the volunteers who took time from their busy schedules to do an initial draft review of this guide.

We cannot forget to acknowledge the County of San Diego, The Regional Community Recovery Team of San Diego, which we were able to participate in after the 2003 and 2007 firestorms in San Diego, and the CRT for their support. Last, but certainly not least, we would like to thank Deena Raver for helping to initiate support for this project.

Background of This Workbook

After George Kehrer lost his home in the 1991 Oakland Hills Fire, he joined an *ad hoc* group appropriately named the "Unexpectedly Underinsured Allstate Policyholders" or UUAP. The media had another name for those affected by the fire – "Disaster Victims."

Although the fire had initially victimized them and their neighborhood, this group soon found themselves pulling out of "victim" mode and into a new "survivor" mentality. Since then we've seen "disaster victims" from around the United States become "disaster survivors." This is how we, throughout this book, refer to those who recover from disaster as we did and as you will too.

These newly branded "survivors" soon learned that for those covered by insurance, getting their claim paid was by far the biggest immediate hurtle they had to clear to move on. Through an extreme stroke of fate, shortly after the Oakland Hills fire, George ran into an ex-adjuster of 20 years named Ina DeLong who was fed up with the tactics used by State Farm against policyholders following the 1989 Loma Prieta Earthquake. She was determined to teach Oakland Hills Fire survivors what she knew about the role of insurance adjusters in the insurance settlement process so disaster survivors could get a fair settlement.

Two years after the Oakland Hills Fire, large wildfires struck Los Angeles County. Ms. DeLong had sufficiently mentored George and he not only credited her with his successful insurance recovery but wanted to pass on the knowledge to this new group of survivors in Southern California and headed there in late 1993. That is how he found himself in the Los Angeles area when, in January of 1994, the Northridge earthquake devastated the San Fernando Valley.

Due to the hundreds of thousands of people now trying to rebuild their homes and lives, San Fernando Valley community leaders decided a local Southern California nonprofit organization devoted to recovering from the Northridge Earthquake was needed. Almost overnight, Community Assisting Recovery, Inc. or CARe, was formed and George was asked to serve as its first executive director.

CARe worked tirelessly for seven years, providing free insurance, construction and other disaster recovery information services to residents and businesses, rooting out building and other scams preying on vulnerable property owners, and fighting for insurance reform. By 2001, insurance claims they had fought to re-open were finally adjusted correctly.

George had only a small break before a large wildfire hit Arizona in 2002, and then the 2003 wildfires again hit Southern California. In the wake of more wildfires in the Southern California in 2007, and then in Santa Barbara in 2008, CARe received much appreciated funding through the San Diego Foundation to publish, in this book, what they've learned over the previous 17 years.

We hope you, the newest Disaster Survivor, find this book helpful in your road to recovery.

Table of Contents

Table of Figures

Forward

On October 25, 2003 I got a call from my brother that I will never forget. He told me our mother's house had just burned to the ground. "To the ground?" I asked, in disbelief. "To the ground," he replied. I lived 120 miles away and hadn't even heard about the wildfires raging out of control in the foothills of the San Bernardino Mountains.

The next day, three fires started in the San Diego area where I lived. My husband had to go to his office on a Sunday to evacuate important documents. Even though we lived miles from the nearest field of brush, I started to pack photo albums in the car. In the end, we were not directly impacted, but my mother found herself included in the more than 4,500 families all over Southern California who were not as fortunate.

During those first couple of weeks following the fire, I started searching the internet for anything that could tell me how I could help my mom. I didn't find much that was useful. Desperate for information, I started a website for my mom describing her situation (in a style that would now be described as a blog). I emailed the link to everyone in my contact list and also shared it with every internet group of which I was a member.

In the meantime, my mom contacted the insurance company. They asked her to create a personal property inventory list and requested that she sign some paperwork, but whether these were indeed the correct next steps, we had no idea. There were many community meetings in the weeks following the wildfires. Officials from government and nonprofit organizations would stand before the assembled and announce: "We're here to help." No one, however, could say exactly what the next step should be or whether we were on the right track.

Luckily someone from one of the online groups read my post and emailed me about a meeting that was taking place in my mother's community. It was billed as "QUESTIONS AND ANSWERS FOR FIRE VICTIMS!" and was being organized by some previous fire survivors. I decided to drive the two hours to attend and found survivors from many other California fires, including the 1990 Oakland Hills Fire (Alameda County), the 1993 Eaton Canyon Fire (Los Angeles County), and the 2002 Pines Fire (San Diego County). I walked away completely energized. The information and understanding they provided was absolutely empowering.

George Kehrer, Executive Director of CARe (Community Assisting Recovery, Inc.) and co-author of this guide, was the main speaker. He helped us start to understand what we needed to do next. He put us on a path to empower ourselves and learn what we needed to do to get almost twice as much from the insurance company as the policy called for.

George inspired me to continue the learning process and pointed the way to thorough research and a multitude of books specifically written for insurance claimants. He gave me the courage to call organizations and ask for information, something I might not have done without him. I found countless sources of free information that I had not been able to find on my own following the fire.

Much was going on in my life at that time, in addition to the fire. Without knowing it, George Kehrer helped build me up and gave me new courage and direction in my life.

I will forever be grateful to him for his drive to help others and for recognizing my determination to do the right thing for my mother. I want to thank him for giving all of this to me, and I want to return the favor by sharing this with you.

Lila Hayes

CARe Board Member and Co-Author

Chapter 1 **Getting Started**

Introduction

We understand this is a stressful time for you. We understand because we have been through it ourselves. We know that right after a disaster, there is too much to learn and not enough time. We know your mind is racing so fast it's hard to grasp all of the new information being thrown at you.

Remember that everyone working for the insurance company has much more experience than the average claimant. This is your chance to become educated so you can play the "claims game" on a more level playing field.

> *"We understand because we have been through it ourselves."*

Imagine if you will that you've never played poker before. You have heard of poker, you are familiar with a deck of cards, and maybe you have even flipped past people playing poker on TV once or twice, but you have never even played a single hand of poker in your life. Now imagine that one day, out of the blue, you are forced to compete in a poker tournament with four highly skilled professional players. On the line? How about your house and everything you own. How do you think you'd do? Would you lose your house? Would you lose everything you've worked for your entire life?

It might seem extreme, but this hypothetical game of poker is not unlike the 'claims game' played with the insurance company following a large property loss. You might be lucky enough to sit at a table with a group of very nice people who teach you the rules and guide you through the entire tournament. Or you might not.

This is not a book on how to rip off the insurance company (or cheat at poker). It is simply a book to help you keep focused and move through the insurance claim process. Remember, it was they who were kind enough to accept your business and write a policy promising to pay for repairs in a situation such as this and we wrote this book to teach you about every penny the insurance company owes you.

First Steps

It is our hope that through this book we can bring you enough information so that you can come to a full and fair settlement and be on your way to recovery.

The biggest challenge for an instruction manual on the insurance claim process is that, like a fingerprint, every claim is unique. Even two claims with the same insurance company and the same adjuster can have significant differences. You will also find that several things will demand your attention simultaneously at a time when you barely have the ability to deal with them individually.

It is with these challenges in mind that we've created this guide to help you through the process.

1. To get started, read "The Claims Process in a Nutshell" on page 3.

2. Review the "Insurance Flow Chart" on page 5 and determine which of these steps you've completed.

3. Use the rest of the book as a reference guide. You can read it all the way through or refer to it when a particular question or concern arises.

4. Use the forms and task list at the beginning of each chapter to make sure you're not forgetting anything.

There will be so much going on that you will quickly lose track if you're not extra careful, so please use the forms and tasks to help you remember what you have and haven't completed.

If you would like additional reading, *Policy Ensurance* by Tony Braga (disasterprepared.net) and *Emotional Recovery After Natural Disasters* by Ilana Singer (c-ctherapy.org) are both highly recommended.

The Ultimate Goal

You should know the ultimate goal of this guide is to help you **value your loss** as accurately and thoroughly as possible and to collect all of the money owed to you by the insurance company. This book will help you keep your claim "CLEAN AND STRONG" so that you can replace your lost property to the full extent to which you are entitled.

> *"...the ultimate goal of this guide is to help you value your loss"*

The first six chapters of this book are designed to help you focus on that overall goal. The last two chapters are intended to provide advice and guidance if you find yourself unable to come to an equitable agreement with your insurance company.

Honesty is the Best Policy

Throughout the claim process, you want the insurance company to be honest in its dealings with you, and you must be completely honest as well.

Keep on your toes and don't let them put a "skeleton in your closet" that can cause you a problem later on. For example, let's say you have a 20-year old TV and the adjuster suggests, "Everyone has a flat screen TV these days. Just put one on your list and no one will question it." The problem here is if the insurance company finds you have fraudulently misrepresented any portion of your claim, they can invalidate your *entire claim*. The adjuster has placed a skeleton in your closet that could be used against you later.

However, you are allowed to make mistakes. If you find something that is incorrect (for example, an item on your inventory list that you now realize you didn't actually have), simply write to the insurance company informing them of the error.

This is Not a Race

You might hear people say that disaster recovery is a marathon, not a sprint. We'd like to suggest that it is not a race at all. A race implies competition. Comparing your recovery to others' to determine a "winner" only results in a false sense of success or failure. Avoid any undue pressure to complete any portion of your claim if you're not ready. You are not required to settle quickly, but you must work on your claim in a timely manner.

Pace yourself. If you find yourself becoming overwhelmed, try breaking the tasks into manageable chunks and keep the process moving forward.

This being said, please be keenly aware of important deadlines. (See "Key Policy Deadlines" on page 33.)

The Claims Process in a Nutshell

If there were one page of this book you should concentrate all of your effort in understanding, this would be that page. Dog ear it, sticky-note it or highlight it in whatever manner you see fit, but the next page and a half summarize the entire process.

It is your job to determine the total amount of your loss. It is the insurance company's job to determine how much of the loss they will cover[1]. Whether or not you are an active participant in the negotiation, the difference between the two amounts will be negotiated.

Unlike that hypothetical poker game mentioned previously, you are not here to "win" or make money on your claim. Your property was either severely damaged or completely destroyed, and your goal should be to be appropriately reimbursed for your loss or to get as close to "break even" as possible.

> *It is your job to determine the total amount of your loss. It is the insurance company's job to determine how much of the loss they will cover.*

How Does a Homeowner Determine a Loss?

Most homeowners instinctively want to rely on the insurance company to help value their loss, correctly assuming that they are experts in the field who do this on a daily basis. The problem is if you let them determine your loss, the results will always be in *their* favor.

Here are the first few steps you can take to get started:

1. Collect names and contact information for your adjuster, his boss and preferably their immediate supervisor. Write the information on the contact list form in Chapter 2.

2. Start a claim diary. (See page 11.)

3. Secure appropriate and comfortable living quarters. (See "Appropriate Temporary Living Arrangements" on page 80.)

4. Get a copy of your entire policy. (See page 16, "Obtain a Copy of Your Entire Policy.")

5. Get your own repair/replacement estimates for all lost property and/or Scope of Loss for your home. (For more on this see "Scope of Loss" on page 29.)

6. Create a personal property list. (See Chapter 6.)

What About the Debris?

Before you begin any cleanup efforts, read "Before You Remove the Debris" on page 17.

Your First Recovery Goals

1. Read and understand your insurance policy, your duties and rights. (See Chapter 4.) Digging deeper will require understanding the interaction between the coverages. Explore this further on page 44.

---

[1] Tony Braga helped synthesise this idea for me in his book Policy Ensurance ©2005. In particular, see page 6 where he says, "The company has the right to determine the amount of their liability; you have the right to determine the amount of your claim. Don't blur this fine line. When you suffer a loss, you are the one to claim how much your policy owes you. This means much more than just reporting your loss, it means actually knowing what to ask for, asking for it, adjusting your differences if possible, and knowing what to do if you reach an impasse. The wait and see approach gives up your authority and places you in a much weaker negotiating position. It is very difficult to re-establish authority once it has been relinquished."

2. Obtain the Scope of Loss (or repair estimate) prepared by the insurance company.

3. Obtain your own Scope of Loss. (See Chapter 3, page 29.)

4. Obtain policy limits.

Long-Term Recovery Goals

Early in the claim you will be given partial compensation, but your long term goal is to a) receive money equal to your policy limits and b) to know the true amount of your loss by getting your own repair estimates. At that point you can compare the two numbers and determine if you're underinsured and whether you want to do anything about it. Read more about underinsurance on page 47.

Many people decide that they would rather move on and not push any further. Others decide the potential additional compensation is worth the time and effort. Both decisions are acceptable. Each homeowner must make the decision that is best for them.

Insurance Flow Chart

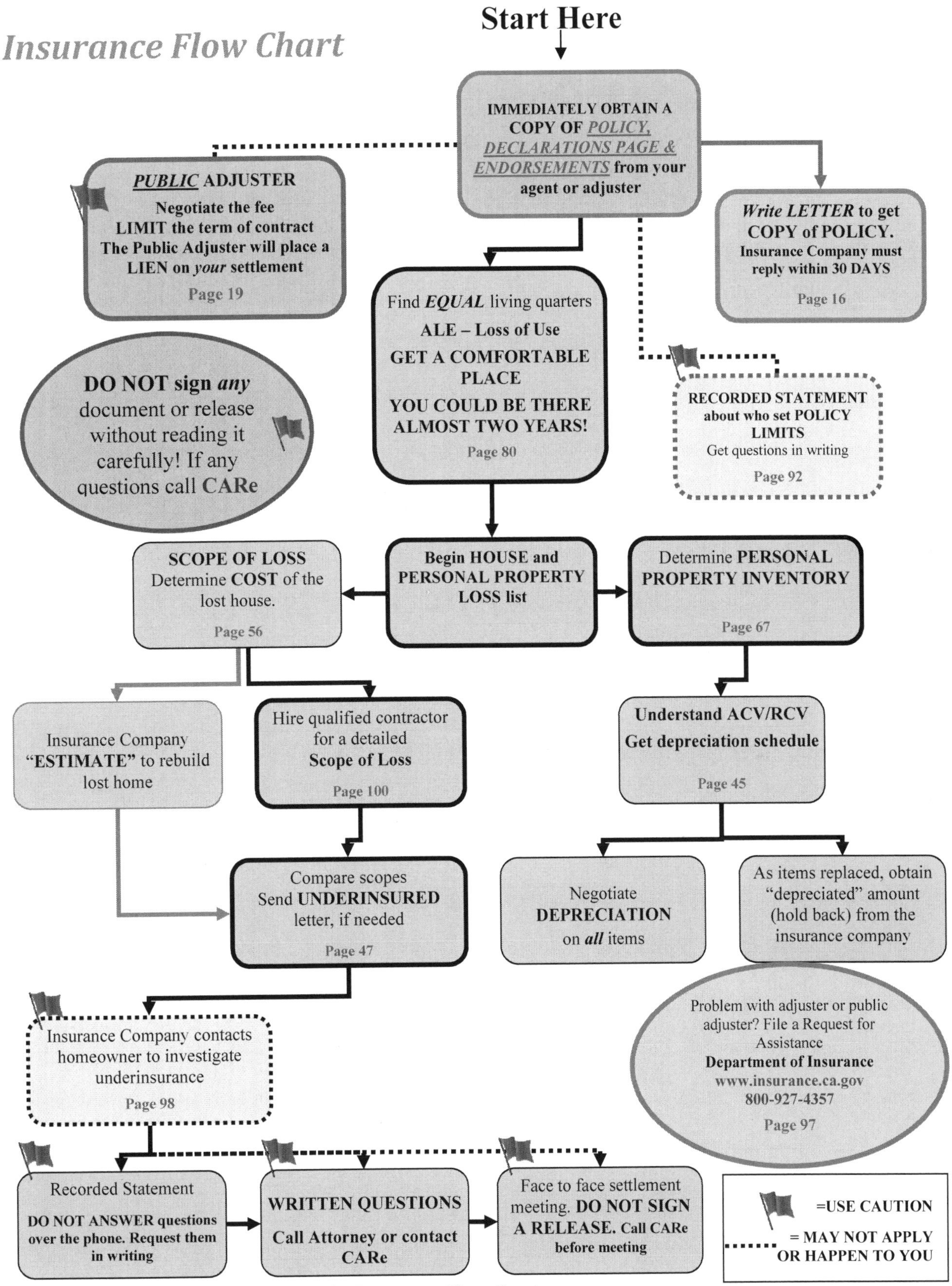

Start Here

IMMEDIATELY OBTAIN A COPY OF *POLICY, DECLARATIONS PAGE & ENDORSEMENTS* from your agent or adjuster

PUBLIC ADJUSTER
Negotiate the fee
LIMIT the term of contract
The Public Adjuster will place a
LIEN on *your* settlement
Page 19

Write LETTER to get COPY of POLICY.
Insurance Company must reply within 30 DAYS
Page 16

DO NOT sign *any* document or release without reading it carefully! If any questions call CARe

Find *EQUAL* living quarters
ALE – Loss of Use
GET A COMFORTABLE PLACE
YOU COULD BE THERE ALMOST TWO YEARS!
Page 80

RECORDED STATEMENT about who set POLICY LIMITS
Get questions in writing
Page 92

SCOPE OF LOSS
Determine **COST** of the lost house.
Page 56

Begin HOUSE and PERSONAL PROPERTY LOSS list

Determine **PERSONAL PROPERTY INVENTORY**
Page 67

Insurance Company **"ESTIMATE"** to rebuild lost home

Hire qualified contractor for a detailed **Scope of Loss**
Page 100

Understand ACV/RCV
Get depreciation schedule
Page 45

Compare scopes
Send **UNDERINSURED** letter, if needed
Page 47

Negotiate **DEPRECIATION** on *all* items

As items replaced, obtain "depreciated" amount (hold back) from the insurance company

Insurance Company contacts homeowner to investigate underinsurance
Page 98

Problem with adjuster or public adjuster? File a Request for Assistance
Department of Insurance
www.insurance.ca.gov
800-927-4357
Page 97

Recorded Statement
DO NOT ANSWER questions over the phone. Request them in writing

WRITTEN QUESTIONS
Call Attorney or contact CARe

Face to face settlement meeting. **DO NOT SIGN A RELEASE. Call CARe** before meeting

=USE CAUTION
= MAY NOT APPLY OR HAPPEN TO YOU

Figure 1: Insurance Flow Chart

Download and print a color copy of this chart from our website www.carehelp.org

Meeting with Other Disaster Survivors

If the disaster you survived affected others as well, you should consider going to (or holding) regular meetings with your fellow survivors to compare notes. It's possible that a group is already forming in your area.

> *"Power in knowledge. Comfort in community. We found these things to be crucial in our fire recovery process."*
>
> *-Linda D.*

As CEO of Community Partners, Paul Vandeventer states in the forward of the workbook *From Chaos to Community*, "…the work of long-term community recovery and rebuilding ultimately falls to the people who plan to go on living in the place where the disaster struck. From the singular effort of rebuilding a home, to the more complex efforts that help neighborhood residents feel safe and stable again, community recovery and rebuilding depends on people joining together."

For tips and information on organizing a community recovery group, you can obtain this workbook free of charge from Community Partners. You can download it from their website at *www.communitypartners.org* or call them for a printed copy at 213-346-3200.

Survivors have also reported that getting together with neighbors helps them feel like they're not alone. For example:

- Linda D., survivor of the 2003 Grand Prix fire in Rancho Cucamonga California said: "Power in knowledge. Comfort in community. We found these things to be crucial in our fire recovery process."

- Barbara R., survivor of the 2007 Witch Fire in San Diego California said: "The meetings also gave [us] an opportunity to confer and commiserate with other fire victims."

- Angela A., who went through the 2008 Tea Fire in Santa Barbara California said: "Last Thursday morning I woke with the feeling that 'I just want someone's hand to hold who knows about all this.' Two hours later I bumped into another fire victim at the post office and he told me about the [community] meeting that night. How cool is that?"

Chapter 2 **First Steps to Recovery**

YOUR CONTACT INFORMATION

Loss Address: _____

_____

Mailing Address: _____

_____

Current Address: _____

_____

Phone Number: _____

Cell Number: _____

Work Number: _____

Fax Number: _____

Email Address: _____

Notes: _____

_____

_____

_____

_____

_____

_____

_____

_____

_____

_____

_____

_____

_____

_____

_____

Other Contacts:

Name: _____Number: _____

Email address: _____

Name: _____Number: _____

Email address: _____

Name: _____Number: _____

Email address: _____

INSURANCE COMPANY INFORMATION

Policy Number:_____   **Claim Number**: _____

Main Office

Company Name: _____

Physical Address: _____

_____

_____

Mailing Address: _____

_____

Phone: _____

Fax: _____

Email: _____

Website: _____

Notes: _____

_____

_____

_____

_____

Agent: _____

Physical Address: _____

_____

_____

Mailing Address: _____

_____

Phone: _____

Fax: _____

Email: _____

Website: _____

Notes: _____

_____

_____

_____

_____

_____

Adjuster #1: _____

Adjuster's Superior: _____

Physical Address: _____

_____

_____

Mailing Address: _____

_____

Phone: _____

Fax: _____

Email: _____

_____

Main Office (in charge of adjusters):

Adjuster's Superior: _____

Physical Address: _____

_____

_____

Mailing Address: _____

_____

Phone: _____

Fax: _____

Email: _____

_____

Adjuster #2: _____

Adjuster's Superior: _____

Physical Address: _____

_____

_____

Mailing Address: _____

_____

Phone: _____

Fax: _____

Email: _____

Tasks for This Chapter

☐ Fill out the information on the first page(s) of this chapter.

☐ Get a copy of your policy.

☐ Get an official payoff letter from your mortgage company.

☐ Start a claim diary.

☐ Purchase items on the shopping list on page 12.

☐ Read about what to do with the checks you're given in the section called "Take the Money" on page 13.

☐ Protect your property from further damage.

☐ Document your loss before you remove the debris.

☐ If considering a public adjuster, read our section titled "Public Adjusters" on page 19.

About Your Policy and Your Claim

You bought an **insurance policy** from your insurance company. It is an agreement that states they promise to pay for certain damages if you pay your premium. Most people hope to never file a claim but feel better knowing the promise is there when needed. Unfortunately, it is needed now. Some people feel bad about taking money from their insurance company, but this is their responsibility and it is why you've been paying the premiums. Don't feel bad using a service for which you've paid money. Regardless of the size of the disaster, insurance companies turn a very significant profit and have plenty of money with which to pay your claim.

When you call to file a claim you will be assigned a **claim number** and an **adjuster** who will be your primary contact during the claim process. An adjuster can either work as an employee of the insurance company or as a contractor on loan from an outside adjusting company. In large disasters, most insurance companies will hire these temporary, independent, outside adjusters due to the high volume of claims in the area. Outside adjusters are not to be confused with public adjusters. Please see page 19 for information on public adjusters.

Some people have an **insurance agent** from whom they purchased their policy. This is the sales person who sells you the policy but is not the person in charge of your claim. Although some agents can be helpful with answering questions about your policy, the **adjuster** is the main contact for your claim.

> *"...the claim process is not something that happens to you. Whether you know or it or not, you direct the action, even if it is simply through your inaction."*

Write your claim number and your adjuster's contact information on the form at the beginning of this chapter. You might notice there is room for several adjusters' names. You can expect to be in contact with several adjusters throughout the life of a large claim, as they often move on for personal reasons or are assigned to other disasters. It is up to you to be organized and to keep track of all of the information as it sometimes falls between the cracks when changing from adjuster to adjuster.

You should also get contact information for your insurance company as you will most likely need to send them correspondence throughout the life of your claim. Make sure you have several ways to get in touch with them, such as a physical address (for UPS/FedEx), mailing address (for US Postal Mail), fax and phone numbers, website and email address.

If you've already filed a claim and haven't gotten all of this information that's perfectly fine. Start making calls now to get all of the information you need.

Remember: the claim process is not something that happens to you. Whether you know or it or not, you direct the action, even if it is simply through your inaction. If you fail to learn about the claim process the adjuster will make the decisions for you, and his decisions might not be in your best interest.

Your Deductible

Policies include what is called a **deductible**. That is the monetary portion of the loss which *you* are obligated to pay. The deductible is usually deducted from the claim amount. For example, if you had a loss of $10,000 and a deductible of $1,000 the insurance company should pay $9,000.

If your loss is beyond your policy limits at least a portion of the deductible is usually waived.

Keep a Claim Diary

A **claim diary** can be as simple as a call log, or as detailed as a blow-by-blow account of everything done during the day. The more detailed you are the better, but you also don't want to add more to your already busy schedule by spending hours writing everything down. You'll have to find a happy medium for yourself, but you *must* at least keep an activity log.

An activity log is simply a list of people you've talked to, whether on the phone or in person. If possible, take notes while you're talking to them, whether you're on the phone or in person. Note the date of contact and maybe even the time. There is so much new information that you are being inundated with, you'll find it will come in very, *very* handy later on.

See also Chapter 3, "Communicating to Protect Your Claim."

Activity Log [sample]

Date	Time	Name	Subject

Shopping List

To help you get organized there are a few things you'll want to purchase from an office supply store. Typically, you will have received an advance on your claim from the insurance company, so now is the time to put that money to good use.

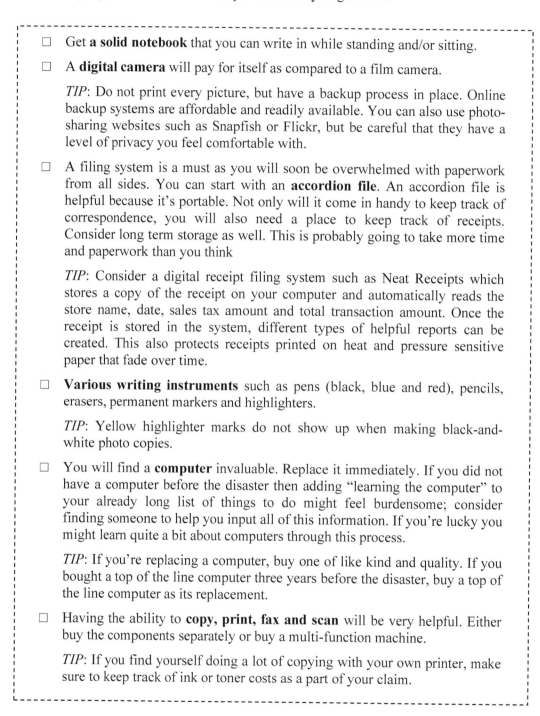

☐ Get **a solid notebook** that you can write in while standing and/or sitting.

☐ A **digital camera** will pay for itself as compared to a film camera.

TIP: Do not print every picture, but have a backup process in place. Online backup systems are affordable and readily available. You can also use photo-sharing websites such as Snapfish or Flickr, but be careful that they have a level of privacy you feel comfortable with.

☐ A filing system is a must as you will soon be overwhelmed with paperwork from all sides. You can start with an **accordion file**. An accordion file is helpful because it's portable. Not only will it come in handy to keep track of correspondence, you will also need a place to keep track of receipts. Consider long term storage as well. This is probably going to take more time and paperwork than you think

TIP: Consider a digital receipt filing system such as Neat Receipts which stores a copy of the receipt on your computer and automatically reads the store name, date, sales tax amount and total transaction amount. Once the receipt is stored in the system, different types of helpful reports can be created. This also protects receipts printed on heat and pressure sensitive paper that fade over time.

☐ **Various writing instruments** such as pens (black, blue and red), pencils, erasers, permanent markers and highlighters.

TIP: Yellow highlighter marks do not show up when making black-and-white photo copies.

☐ You will find a **computer** invaluable. Replace it immediately. If you did not have a computer before the disaster then adding "learning the computer" to your already long list of things to do might feel burdensome; consider finding someone to help you input all of this information. If you're lucky you might learn quite a bit about computers through this process.

TIP: If you're replacing a computer, buy one of like kind and quality. If you bought a top of the line computer three years before the disaster, buy a top of the line computer as its replacement.

☐ Having the ability to **copy, print, fax and scan** will be very helpful. Either buy the components separately or buy a multi-function machine.

TIP: If you find yourself doing a lot of copying with your own printer, make sure to keep track of ink or toner costs as a part of your claim.

Take the Money

It is not uncommon for your insurance adjuster to begin offering you partial financial compensation from the outset, particularly when there has been a total loss following a disaster and there are few questions about the cause of the loss.

Some claimants are hesitant to take insurance company checks if they know it won't cover the entire loss. Money that comes to you is *not* to be considered payment in full unless that fact is explicitly stated in the paperwork you receive with the check. **DO** take the money, but **DO NOT** sign a release on the spot, including a **Proof of Loss** (see page 29 for more information on the Proof of Loss). Even if you're told the adjusters can "choose" to re-open your claim, this is solely at their discretion. Any release you sign can mean the **END** of your claim. If the insurance company gives you a check that says "final payment" or includes a release in an accompanying letter, tell them to re-issue a check without such wording and to revoke the release in writing.

> *"If the insurance company gives you a check that says 'final payment' ... tell them to re-issue a check without such wording."*

You should not feel pressured to sign anything without taking the time to look it over. If you need time to process what is presented to you, make it a practice to tell your adjuster you will review the documents and get back to them.

Make a copy of both sides of every check you receive. Keep a log and a copy of the checks.

Keep your money in a safe place. **Do not place your money in an uninsured account.** This money is to be considered *short-term savings*. Do not risk it by playing with risky investments.

Mortgage Company on the Check

Some people are surprised to find the mortgage company's name on an insurance company issued check. There is a clause in the policy that states that the mortgage company's name will be on any insurance payments if there is a loss on the dwelling which is more than a certain amount (commonly $10,000). The mortgage company has a vested interest in the house and wants some sort of guarantee that you'll invest the money back into the house and not on something personal like an extended international vacation.

Other payments that might include the mortgage company's name are for landscape and other structures (more on these coverages in Chapter 7).

On the other hand, property that the mortgage company does not have an interest in should *not* have the mortgage company's name on it. These coverages include personal property (Chapter 6) and loss of use (Chapter 7).

What do I need to do with the dwelling check(s)?

1. Do not endorse a check to the lender until you know how the bank is going to handle funding the reconstruction of your home.

2. Call the mortgage company. Get a copy of their procedure detailing how they will release the funds.

3. Once you sign the check over to the bank, you have lost any power you may have in negotiating any modifications of the bank's procedures. It is possible you have no real power in changing their procedure, but the only way to know is by hanging on to the check while you discuss with the bank any problems you may foresee with their construction funding procedure.

4. You may have to climb the chain of command before you find someone at the lending institution who will listen to your questions or has the authority to negotiate.

5. DO NOT HESITATE TO REMIND THE BANK OF YOUR FIRE LOSS STATUS. Your fire loss should put you near the head of any line.

What if my loan amount is less than the insurance company payment?

1. Get an official loan payoff letter from your bank as soon as possible that states the payoff amount of your loan.

2. Send a copy of the letter to your adjuster and make a request in writing to receive a check in the amount of the loan payable to both you and the bank. Also request the balance and any subsequent checks payable to you only.

3. If you already have a check that exceeds the loan amount, send a photocopy of the check and the bank's payoff amount letter to the adjuster and request in writing that two new checks be issued – one check payable to both you and the bank for the payoff amount; the second for the remaining balance payable to you only. The adjuster may balk at this request, so you may have to be firm and insistent to get the adjuster's understanding and assistance.

4. The loan payoff letter is important to have on file with your insurance adjuster down the line when more settlement funds are made available and you want some control over the incidental expenses in reconstructing your lost or damaged home.

Should I pay off my loan?

1. You should not voluntarily pay off your loan if you anticipate you may need an SBA loan.[2] The SBA may disqualify you, assuming you have your own monetary resources and therefore do not need the Small Business Administration's assistance. Policies constantly change so talk to an SBA representative for more information.

2. If you want to pay off your note and still qualify for SBA funds, ask your lender for a "demand" letter to pay off your loan.

3. Do not pay off your loan if it will make you less qualified for a construction or replacement home loan later when you reapply for lending.

4. The bank procedures for withdrawing insurance money might seem onerous, but the restrictions of working with a construction loan may be even *more* onerous. Research thoroughly before deciding.

5. Paying off the loan might have tax consequences or start the clock ticking for other non-insurance related matters. Contact a CPA for more information.

Is there anything else I should say while talking with my bank?

1. Yes. Ask if they will put your money in at least a 2 percent interest bearing trust account. If the bank is chartered in California it is required by statute to pay at least 2 percent interest. If the bank is federally chartered, it is not required but you can always ask while you still hold the check.

2. Anytime you need a modification in the terms of your loan to meet difficult conditions, such as the serious loss you sustained, ask for the bank's *forbearance* – a legal term for a kind of lending mercy. Temporarily reducing the monthly payment to interest only, or suspending payment for several months, is a form of forbearance.

3. MAKE SURE THE BANK RECORDS AND PUTS IN WRITING ANY CHANGES TO YOUR LOAN.

---

[2] For more information about SBA loans following a disaster, please visit your local disaster recovery center or go to their website at *www.sba.gov* and search for "disaster loans."

4. BEWARE OF ANY TEMPORARY SUSPENSION OF LOAN PAYMENTS. We have received a few reports of payment default and ensuing foreclosure due to a bank's mishandling of the forbearance. The previously approved temporary cessation of loan payments were recorded as simply unpaid and then erroneously sent to the collections department.

5. Keep your own copies of any agreements or changes made.

What else should I do with my insurance checks?

1. Write "PARTIAL PAYMENT" above your endorsement on the back of all checks.

2. After you have signed the check, PHOTOCOPY front and back and save (in your filing system) both sides of all checks you are given.

3. DO NOT NEGOTIATE any check that states or infers the payment is FINAL unless you are absolutely certain that your entire insured loss has been determined and is being paid. Otherwise, you may jeopardize any underinsurance or settlement issues you have or may discover at a later date.

4. Have the insurer reissue any check that states or infers a FINAL payment, removing or deleting the statement or inference.

Obtain a Copy of Your Entire Policy

Since your **insurance policy** will determine how much money you will receive from the insurance company, the first thing you need to do is get a copy of it. You can call your agent, your adjuster and the head office and request a copy, but you also need to request a copy in writing. According to California state law, the insurance company has 60 days to send you a copy once you request it, but you will need proof that you actually requested the policy. Not responding to these policy requests is one of the most common complaints we hear after a major disaster.

Think of this policy as something like a "rule book" for a poker game. You could rely on the other people at the table to tell you the rules, but you would have nothing to verify that what they're saying is accurate.

The policy is a long, legal document that details all of the ins and outs of the agreement between you and the insurance company. The policy is usually dozens of pages long and it comes in three sections:

1. **Declarations page**: Usually only one or two pages long. It looks a lot like the billing page you get annually in the mail when you pay your premium.

2. **Policy**: This sometimes comes in a bound or stapled booklet format with tissue-paper thin pages and makes up the bulk of your policy packet.

3. **Endorsements**: This section can also be very lengthy and changes the policy for various reasons, such as when you buy extra coverage for certain items, or when the state makes a law that changes the policy. The number of endorsements you have will be spelled out on your declarations page. (See Chapter 4 for more information about your policy.)

Unfortunately, for the average homeowner the policy can be very difficult to read. You may have one understanding, but the adjuster might tell you something completely different. They might also ask you to do things that aren't required or clearly spelled out in the policy. See Chapter 4 for how to handle situations like this and more detail about understanding your policy.

Policy Request Sample Letter

[POLICY NUMBER] & [CLAIM NUMBER]

Dear [ADJUSTER/INSURANCE COMPANY NAME]:

As you are aware, we lost our home and everything in it during the [**DISASTER**].

We also lost our copy of our insurance policy, endorsements and the declarations page.

We have requested a copy of our insurance policy, endorsements and declaration page several times from both our adjuster and agent. We have never received it. [**IF APPLICABLE**]

We also learned from the California Homeowners Bill of Rights that we are entitled to a copy of our policy and declarations page. Please send us immediately an accurate copy of our policy, including all endorsements and our declarations page.

If you have any problems, please let us know in writing immediately, but no later than 15 days.

Sincerely,

[Homeowner signature] & [Homeowner NAME]

Protect Your Property from Further Damage

One of the first things that the policy requires of you is to **mitigate your damages**. What this means is that you have to take every reasonable step to make sure that more damage does not occur to your property or that you aren't exposed to a liability claim by not protecting your property from new dangers.

If your house is still partially standing, you should have a contractor immediately come and make temporary arrangements to protect what is still standing. This might mean tarps on the roof or boarding up certain parts of the house. It could also require temporary fencing around the property to protect against liability (for example, someone falling into an open pool or tripping over the rubble).

Damage Mitigation Check List:

☐ Are there any holes or deep pits that need to be covered or protected?

☐ Is there any property left on the lot that you want to keep? If so, remove or securely store it to protect it from theft.

☐ Is there anything on the property that can be damaged by water, including rain?

☐ Do you need to protect against debris flow?

Before You Remove the Debris

Most people assume that the first thing you should do with the debris on your land is to remove it. However, if you do this before going through the process of documenting your loss, you could easily shortchange yourself. Documentation prepared by the insurance company might not be enough proof to demonstrate your full loss.

Before your debris is removed – and if you want to preserve your ability to achieve a full and fair settlement of your loss – you must do some quick but careful research to answer questions your insurance company will have regarding the size of your home, the quality of your house construction, and other personal property.

Once you sign a debris removal contract you may lose your right to control the actual date of debris removal. The lot may be cleared without notice and before you have completed your documentation. If you have already authorized debris removal, request a postponement to give yourself time to retrieve evidence of lost possessions, construction elements and building dimensions.

> *"...if you [remove the debris] before going through the process of documenting your loss, you could easily shortchange yourself."*

For best results, we recommend that you do not remove your debris until your adjuster has given you a Scope of Loss or detailed construction estimate. It is at this point you will know if issues exist that require access to the dwelling site, the building footings and foundation, and debris.

You should be aware that some counties place deadlines on when the lot has to be cleared, but you should be able to request an extension. Other counties might implement debris removal programs. Be careful about jumping the gun on signing up for one of these programs as you might lose control of the project and have very little recourse.

Before Your Land is Cleared You Must Measure, Photograph and Save

Measure

1. Measure the slab or the perimeter of each structure. It might even be helpful to have someone video while you're measuring, and then zoom in on the measurement so it is readable. You'd be amazed at how important documenting the size of your dwelling

can become. Survivors can be shortchanged on the replacement cost as a result of inadequate measurements.

2. Focus on the height and thickness of the footings, stem walls, any slab and chimney.

3. Although you can also use satellite photos to locate your house on the property, you should also measure how far the house is from the property line or other permanent landmark (such as a telephone pole or a very old tree). For best results, measure the same spot on the house from two different landmarks.

Photograph

1. Take pictures of everything. A digital camera can be very helpful since you don't have to pay to develop every picture, and you will have a continual supply of "reprints" should an adjuster lose the ones you send. A video camera might also be helpful. Many digital cameras and cell phones now record video, but the low quality might make it less useful.

2. Take as many photos as you can. You can never take too many.

3. Include a ruler, yardstick or tape measure to document dimensions in the photograph.

Save

1. Go to your lot with a rake and large container, breathing mask and gloves. If, for whatever reason, you are unable to do this, recruit friends or family to handle the task.

2. Carefully poke through the ash to recover and SAVE in the container any small remnants of tile, pieces of metal, copper piping, wood scraps – any tangible items to prove to your insurance company the quality of items and construction you had. You will be surprised how much is buried in the ash.

3. Keep the saved items in a safe place to show to your current and subsequent adjusters the quality of materials, workmanship and possessions you had. You want to be able to provide evidence that will support claims such as the kind of tile that was in place, the types of light fixtures you had, the type of wood used, or what the foundation was like.

Public Adjusters

A **public adjuster** is a professional who the homeowner may decide to hire to serve as the middleman between themselves and the insurance company. A public adjuster can charge a fee ranging from 4 percent to 30 percent or more of your insurance claim. A public adjuster is licensed and regulated by your state.

To seel their service, they claim that you'll have to do less work and will probably get more money for your claim because of their experience and expertise around the insurance settlement process. A drawback, however, is that they cannot practice law and will have to hire a lawyer or other professionals (usually for an additional fee) if that need arises.

> *"If you have a loss that exceeds your policy limit, a public adjuster will not be able to get more without involving legal assistance."*

Unfortunately, they will still need you to document your loss. It was your house and you'll still have to provide from memory or sift through debris to determine what you had. You might find yourself doing much more paperwork than you bargained for. From our experience, in most cases the amount of work they do is not nearly worth the money they charge.

Also, if you have a loss that exceeds your policy limit, a public adjuster *will not* be able to get you more money without involving legal assistance. It is a good idea to see how far you can get *on your own* before hiring *any* professional.

Even with the public adjuster running interference between you and the insurance company you still must be 100 percent involved in the process. Only you know the true extent of your loss. The public adjuster may offer to give you the "inside dope" on the insurance claims settlement process, but most fire survivors can handle all the paperwork themselves. With the Internet at your fingertips and advocacy groups ready to help, all you will really need to settle your claim is available for free.

If you are still thinking about hiring a public adjuster, please consider the following:

1. Disregard the sales pitch. A big portion of your future financial security depends on the skill and knowledge of the public adjuster you may hire. Select the person as carefully as you would your doctor, lawyer, CPA or investment counselor. Check the public adjuster's license qualifications, certifications or complaints on your state's department of insurance website.

2. If hired, the public adjuster's name will appear on your insurance checks. A public adjuster will place a lien on your insurance claim, which means the public adjuster will be a payee on all your insurance settlement checks. What's more, a public adjuster may even keep a lien on your settlement long after working on your claim and even after you terminate the contract or take legal action against your insurance company.

3. From our experience, we have seen insurance company adjusters become more stringent with the policy requirements once a public adjuster is hired. While not the fault of the public adjuster, the result can place an extra burden on the homeowner who must now be ever more vigilant in proceeding with the settlement process.

4. The public adjuster – NOT YOU – controls your claim.

5. The public adjuster selects the "experts" who determine the value of your claim.

6. The public adjuster may sell your claim short because of a heavy workload or another disaster.

7. A public adjuster CANNOT handle legal issues regarding your claim.

8. The public adjuster you initially meet with may be more of a "salesperson" and your claim may be handled by a different, less experienced public adjuster.

9. Insurance companies will NOT pay the fees and costs of your public adjuster.

Use the following strategies and information to protect your rights:

1. Do as much as you can on your own. Limit the contract to funds you have not or cannot get on your own.

2. Be certain the public adjuster with whom you sign will actually work your claim. Some may assign your claim to a less qualified person.

3. Make sure you get copies of ALL communications between your insurance company and public adjusters. We have had complaints that Proofs of Loss and other important documents were processed and signed by the public adjuster but never seen by the homeowner.

4. Avoid single practitioner or small public adjuster firms unless they can demonstrate they have the personnel and track record to handle your claim to its satisfactory completion.

5. Negotiate the fee. As in any contract, fees are negotiable.

6. Limit the term of the contract to no more than six months. If the public adjuster cannot do the job within six months of your loss, you don't need the public adjuster.

7. Verify that the public adjuster removes any lien once the contract is terminated.

8. Before you sign anything, determine how long you have to cancel the contract without fee or penalty.

If you have any reservations, use your right to cancel the contract. If you change your mind and can't do the work yourself you can always go back to them later.

Commonly Overlooked Damage

Insurance adjusters are infamous for "not seeing" less visible damage, and using "cosmetic" techniques to avoid the higher costs of necessary repairs or replacements. Shortcuts intended to rid odor, contamination or corrosion from damaged property may ultimately prove unsatisfactory; in some cases replacement may be the only option.

If you notice additional damage, or if damage returns (even if it's a year later), call your insurance company to finish or continue repairs or replacement.

In the case of partial damage, the "Line of Sight Rule" is especially applicable. (Please see page 62.)

If you find that left over (and sometimes invisible) debris or traces of smoke is making you sick even after repairs have been made, it is *not* repaired to its pre-loss condition.

> *"Shortcuts intended to rid odor, contamination or corrosion from damaged property may ultimately prove unsatisfactory."*

All Claims

The following are often overlooked during the claim process:

1. Asbestos report. You might need one during debris removal; look for coverage to pay for one.

2. Damage resulting from repair work. California Insurance Code §2695.9(a)(1) states:

   "When a loss requires repair or replacement of an item or part, any consequential physical damage incurred in making the repair or replacement not otherwise excluded by the policy shall be included in the loss. The insured shall not have to pay for depreciation nor any other cost except for the applicable deductible."

3. A soils report might be needed when rebuilding. Soil disturbed by debris removal or earthquake-damaged soils can affect the stability of your building.

Special Considerations for Partial Losses

Cleaning and repair of personal property for a partial loss claim can quickly turn into a huge headache. Be sure to reference page 76 for some tips survivors have reported helped them through the process.

If there is anything on your property that is partially damaged, the **Line of Sight** rule will come into play during the insurance claim process. Please see page 62 for more information on the "Line of Sight Rule."

Earthquake

Look for these things as you work to determine the full extent of your loss:

1. Sound structure. This may require an engineering report.

2. Concrete slab cracks. Did the adjuster look under the carpets?

3. Framing damage.

4. Unlevel floors.

5. Doors and windows out of square or sticking.

6. Loose mortar or cracked chimney — inside or out.

7. Stucco, plaster or drywall cracks.

8. Loose or cracked attic rafters, trusses or ridge boards. Did the adjuster ever look in the attic with a powerful light?

9. Leaks or damage to roofing or sheathing.

10. Shower tile cracks or leaks.

11. Water or sewer pipe leaks.

Fire (Partial losses)

Inspect these things to help determine the full extent of your loss:

Exterior

1. Concrete foundations, slabs, retaining walls, sidewalks and patios

   a) Concrete may dehydrate and weaken. Discoloration, spalling (flaking) and cracks indicate damage. *Never* reuse a slab without extensive inspections. A slab can retain the smell of smoke for many years; they are rarely re-usable.

   b) Mortars, adhesives and sealants may be weakened and lose integrity.

2. Stucco and siding

   a) Stucco may dehydrate and over time, spall and/or crack.

   b) Siding may melt, distort or become brittle.

   c) Siding may be pock-marked by burning embers or chemical sprays.

3. Aluminum and other metals

   a) Aluminum, steel, iron and other metals can expand, deform and corrode.

   b) Embedded metal, rebar and pipes can expand and crack concrete slabs, foundations and retaining walls.

4. Roofing

   a) Burning embers create small holes and pock-marked surfaces which can result in leaks and discoloration.

   b) The waterproof membrane and roof structure beneath can be compromised.

   c) Investigate further if you find leaks later.

5. Windows

   a) Window frames may melt, corrode, blister and/or discolor.

   b) Glass may corrode, warp, discolor and/or lose some clarity.

   c) Dual pane glass may lose the vacuum seal. You might not realize this until you see a fine mist appear in between the panes of glass.

6. Landscaping

   a) Plants may be killed immediately by heat or slowly destroyed by acidic ash.

   b) Soil may be contaminated by chemicals in the wildfire soot.

7. Fire retardants, chemicals and water

   a) Saltwater and chlorinated swimming pool water dropped on your structure can damage such building elements as aluminum, brass and other metals.

   b) Retardants and chemicals, although considered safe, can still damage wood, plastics and metals once exposed to heat, water and/or sun.

Interior

1. Smoke and caustic gases can contaminate porous materials such as fabrics and unfinished wood

   a) Rugs and other interior "soft goods" may be contaminated and/or become brittle.

   b) Carpets can have hidden damage and the odor can seep into the padding.

   c) Ash may leech back up into carpet leaving stains that continually reappear.

   d) Marble, granite and tile may discolor and/or corrode.

   e) Insulation, in the attic and behind the drywall, through openings such as electrical fixtures, absorbs and then may emit fire odors.

2. Ash might reappear on windowsills or you might find it piled up in corners or under electrical outlets. This might indicate additional investigation and/or cleaning is in order.

3. Clothing and linens.

   a) Cloth becomes brittle and loses some, if not most, of its life through various treatments, including ozone, to remove fire odors. (See "Problems Associated with Cleaning Smoke Damaged Items" on page 24.)

   b) Chemicals applied to fabrics to remove odors can cause significant irritation to skin.

4. Consumables

   a) Dry good packages may be contaminated by smoke, ash and caustic gases.

   b) Refrigerated goods may spoil from power interruptions and failures.

5. Appliances and electronics

   a) Refrigerators can be permanently damaged by spoiled food odors resulting from power outages lasting only a few days. Permanent odors like these will require a new refrigerator.

   b) Appliances may be contaminated by chemicals in smoke and soot.

   c) Circuit boards in appliances and electronics are extremely sensitive to chemicals from ash and are highly susceptible to damage.

6. Electrical

   a) Intermittent power interruptions can cause irreparable damage from sparking, arcing and surges in electrical components and circuit boards.

   b) Smoke fumes and ash penetrate into electrical light switch and plug boxes, and even into the wall cavities, requiring removal of odors from drywall and insulation.

7. Plaster and Sheetrock

   a) Plaster is weakened by heat and water.

   b) Sheetrock is degraded by water and loses much, if not all, of its fire resistant qualities.

8. Plumbing

    a) Septic systems often deteriorate from prolonged periods of disuse occurring when a home is unoccupied during repairs.

    b) Septic systems can also be damaged by being driven over by construction vehicles.

9. Heating (HVAC) systems

    a) Soot or ash is blown or drawn into the exterior unit causing contamination.

    b) Ducting may be contaminated by intrusion of soot and ash.

Wind-Driven Rain

Consider the following to make sure your house is repaired to pre-loss condition:

Wind is turbulent and circular; it pulls and sucks with incredible pressure. Drive down the freeway at 65 mph and put your hand out the window. Try it at 90 mph and you'll really notice the difference. Expect the unexpected.

1. In a big storm the roof might lift and damage the entire house. The house has been in a collision with large winds which might cause more damage than what you physically see. Adjusters will rarely see more than what you see.

2. Walls can be lifted off the slab. If a wall is open, look to see if anchor bolts have been lifted and/or loosened, or if the wood beneath the nut is compressed.

3. Foundation damage is possible due to different circumstances during a storm including pressure when the roof and walls were lifted. Have it checked.

4. At night, turn lights off and roll a flashlight flat against the surface to see if there is any twisting or deformation in either direction, or nails popping.

5. Sheetrock is degraded by water and loses its fire resistant qualities.

Consider looking over the list of earthquake damages since strong winds might produce some of the same results.

Problems Associated with Cleaning Smoke Damaged Items

Research on damage caused by smoke and caustic ash reveal a few resources that might prove helpful.

- Stanford University article about recovering objects after a fire includes an interesting section on what smoke really is and how corrosive it can be. Though written for institutions such as libraries and museums, the information can be translated to the home. This piece is especially helpful because it talks about clothes (in the form of costumes), wood furniture, upholstered furniture, books, paintings, etc.:
  http://cool-palimpsest.stanford.edu/byauth/trinkley/wildfire.html

- Article published after 9/11 regarding cleaning objects covered in dust and ash. I freely admit that the kind of dust and ash mentioned in this article is NOT the same as the ash after a wildfire, but it still might prove useful:
  http://www.heritagepreservation.org/PDFS/Dustpressrelease.pdf

- Video on returning to your house after a fire and how to clean possessions:
  http://www.heritagepreservation.org/video/HPsoot.html

- Here are some other links for cleaning fire damaged video tapes, photographic and audio materials:
  www.nfsa.gov.au/preservation/care/first-aid-fire-damaged-audiovisual-materials

Though ozone is widely promoted by ozone-generating equipment companies and cleaning services"[3] as a way to "clean" items damaged by smoke, the side effects of the process should be further explored:

- Ozone "may react with (oxidize) many materials found indoors, including carpets, carpet padding (especially rubber), other floor coverings, furniture, furniture cushion foam, and even surface paints and finishes" and "may in fact generate a second generation of unpleasant and even dangerous outgassing which may remain, persistent indoors, after the ozone 'treatment.'" Check out the following related link:
http://www.inspectapedia.com/sickhouse/OzoneHazards.htm

- This website also has information on the damaging effects of ozone:
http://www.patrickkingassociates.com/effects_of_ozone.htm

Special Considerations for Condo Owners and Other Homeowner Associations

Get a copy of your **homeowner association's bylaws** to verify what is covered by the association's master insurance policy and what is covered by your policy.

1. For condo owners, the HOA generally covers damage to exterior walls and finishes while the condo owner covers damage to the interior walls and finishes.

   (For instance, some condo owners in Tierrasanta, California after the 2003 Southern California wildfires were surprised to return home after the HOA was 'finished' with its portion of the rebuild to find unfinished sub floors, unprimed drywall and no cabinetry. The building department will not allow occupancy of a condo in this condition. It was up to the condo owner to finish the job.)

2. Each HOA is different. Some cover the entire front yard and others don't. Some might even cover the front yard sprinkler system. You'll need to check your own bylaws to figure out what is covered by whom in your HOA.

> "Some insurance policies will have some coverage to pay for an association's assessment, so it's definitely worth looking into."

3. HOA's are almost always responsible for common areas (such as paths, pools and club houses), although they may be able to charge you an *assessment* to cover common area repairs. Some insurance policies will have some coverage ($5,000 to $10,000) to pay for an association's assessment, so it's definitely worth looking into.

---

[3] 7/5/11. http://www.inspectapedia.com/sickhouse/OzoneHazards.htm

Chapter 3 **Starting the Claims Process**

YOUR SPECIALISTS[4]:

Personal Property Specialist: _____

Scope of Loss Expert: _____

Structural Engineer: _____

Architect: _____

Interior Designer: _____

General Contractor: _____

Landscape Contractor: _____

CPA/ Disaster Tax Specialist: _____

Attorney: _____

Other: _____

Other: _____

Other: _____

Other: _____

Other: _____

Insurance adjuster: (See chapter 1 for insurance information)

Notes:

_____

_____

_____

_____

_____

_____

_____

_____

_____

_____

_____

_____

_____

_____

_____

---

[4] These are examples of the experts you may need. Your list may vary.

Tasks For This Chapter

☐ Start creating a list of lost personal items you can recall.

☐ Start looking for a qualified construction professional to help you with a Scope of Loss.

☐ Read the section called "Communicating to Protect Your Claim."

☐ If you think you might be subject to the 180-Day "Replacement" Provision discussed on page 33, write a letter asking your insurance company to waive this deadline.

☐ Mark your calendar for nine months after the loss date as a benchmark and reminder to review your situation. This is when you will determine if you need to contact an attorney and when you will contact your insurance company asking when the one-year deadline for filing suit occurs for your claim.

Your Personal Property Inventory

A **Personal Property Inventory** is an exhaustive list of every item in your home that is not related to the structure. Think of it as a list of everything you *could have* taken with you if you had voluntarily moved from your house. There is no time like the present to start this list. It is a difficult task, but it is in your best interest to start immediately.

Insurance companies count on your forgetfulness. They also know that stress accelerates memory loss. So, before the stresses of your loss start cutting into your memory database, start jotting down personal property items – big things, small things, anything – they all add up to more settlement money in your pocket faster.

Creating an inventory is a long project that requires its own chapter. We have dedicated Chapter 6 for this purpose.

Scope of Loss

After your insurance contract (policy) and your insurance Declarations Page, the **Scope of Loss** is probably **the most important document needed to receive a fair and full settlement** following an insured loss.

Developing a Scope of Loss is similar in detail to developing your personal property inventory. It is a detailed itemization of the quantity and quality of every component of your lost home. In addition, it includes every construction expense (see page 57 "General Conditions") necessary to replicate your lost home.

Your claim representative (insurance company adjuster) probably forgot to tell you that ALL of your other insurance coverage amounts are dependent upon your one Scope of Loss number. If the final Scope of Loss number is less than the *real* cost to replace your loss, every other settlement category amount you receive could end up being too low. (See "The Relationship Between the Coverages" on page 44 for more information.)

More on the Scope of Loss and why it is one of the most important documents you will need for your settlement is covered in Chapter 5.

Hire Your Own Experts

President Ronald Reagan was known to quote a Russian proverb, "Trust, but verify." The insurance company hires their own experts to support their side of the story and you should do the same.

> "Many insureds will either accept what they are being told or will seek advice from someone in the insurance industry or from a lawyer who doesn't specialize in this field. As a result, many legitimate claims go either unpaid or severely underpaid."[5]

Be careful though, of whom you go to for advice. Even within the legal community there are experts in different fields. Just as you wouldn't go to a podiatrist if you had cancer, don't go to your family attorney with questions about insurance.

"Trust, but verify."

-Russian Proverb

If the insurance company treats you unfairly, they are considered to be acting in "bad faith." An attorney who specializes in helping policyholders defend their rights against their insurance company is called an insurance "bad faith" attorney.

Even if you are an attorney yourself, you should also get the opinion of an attorney without connections to your situation – especially if you are an attorney without a

---

[5] 8/12/10. http://www.badfaithinsurance.org/reference/General/0007a.htm

specialization in bad faith. (See Chapter 9 "Hiring Professionals to Help with Your Claim")

Proof of Loss

A **Proof of Loss** is a document sometimes required by the insurance company that lists the total dollar amounts of the damage you sustained broken down by insurance category. Do not confuse this dollar amount with the insurance coverage amounts. You sign this document (almost always in front of a notary) swearing that those dollar amounts are the full and final amounts of your loss. Do not confuse this document with a "Scope of Loss" which is a detailed list of the things you lost within one category (usually referring to your dwelling).

Most policies require that you sign a **Sworn Statement in Proof of Loss** within 60 days following the loss or after a written request is received from your insurance company. In many major disasters, this requirement is waived by the insurance company. However, if it is not waived, you do not have to give away any rights, particularly if a serious issue of underinsurance exists with your loss.

> *Should you receive a Proof of Loss, inform the claim representative that you do not know the loss amounts, but are currently working to gather the information necessary to determine your entire loss.*

After a large loss, many people do not know for several months, or even a year or more, the dollar value of their losses. People continue to remember lost items months down the road. Request, in writing, that your insurance company waive the 60-day Proof of Loss requirement. If the claim representative refuses to waive the requirement, *inform the claim representative that you do not know the loss amounts, but are currently working to gather the information necessary to determine your entire loss.*

Under any circumstances, do NOT ignore the Proof of Loss. Keep a copy of any Proof of Loss, whether you submit one or not.

If you already signed a Proof of Loss do not worry. Continue resolving your claim and make any necessary changes on any new Sworn Statement in Proof of Loss. (If you forgot to keep a copy of the Proof of Loss, request a copy in writing.)

A signed Sworn Statement in Proof of Loss is a legal document that could finalize your insurance settlement by establishing, with FINALITY, your recoverable insured losses. Some Proof of Loss forms state "Partial" on them, but be certain that the entire document is clearly written for a partial payment unless and until you know your total, actual, complete loss.

To prevent accidental or unintended closing or finalizing of your claim, review any Proof of Loss carefully. Some adjusters say "Not to worry," "Tear it up," or "It's only a partial loss sworn statement." However, to keep your claim open and make sure that you don't mistakenly finalize it, you'll want to make a few amendments to your sworn Statement in Proof of Loss, EVEN IF THE ADJUSTER TELLS YOU NOT TO WRITE ON THE DOCUMENT. The following is suggested language to use to assure your Proof of Loss remains open-ended while you continue to determine your actual loss:

- "Partial loss" in front of any dollar amount entered for a given loss
- "Minimum loss" in front of dollar amount
- "At least" in front of dollar amount
- "Loss yet to be determined"
- "Actual loss unknown but at least" in front of dollar amount
- Initial all insertions you make on the Proof of Loss

Other actions to consider:

- Do NOT sign a release when meeting with your adjuster unless you are completely satisfied with your settlement amount.

- ALWAYS give yourself a waiting period before signing any document – at least overnight.

- Document and get repair or replacement estimates for your entire loss including a Scope of Loss for your home and your personal property inventory.

The Role of the Adjuster

In a perfect world, the **insurance adjuster** would help you understand the policy, walk you through the process, make sure you get the checks from the insurance company in a timely manner, and let you know exactly what needs to be done to assure you receive your maximum settlement amount.

In the real world, however, the insurance adjuster is an agent of the company and is their first defense against paying claims (*aka* keeping returns high for their shareholders). Although we recommend on page 29 that you hire your own experts, only a limited number of people can benefit by hiring their own public adjuster. You should read the section on page 19 called "Public Adjusters" before making this decision.

The insurance adjuster is the one who determines how much the insurance company will pay you for your claim. It is *your* responsibility to determine how much you actually lost; it is the adjuster's role to determine not how much you lost, but just how much of your loss the insurance company is willing to pay. This potential power to apply economic pressure at a time when individuals are at their most vulnerable is why most insurance regulation (including those measures addressing "bad faith") exists.

> *"The insurance adjuster is the one who determines how much the insurance company will pay you for your claim. It is your responsibility to determine how much you actually lost."*

Remember that how you relate to the adjuster is a significant factor in how smoothly the claims process will proceed. Unfortunately, personality can drive this process and conflicts can occur. Although in this situation it might be difficult, try not to take it personally:

> "… being timid and allowing yourself to be easily compromised because the adjuster appears to be in a hurry to close his or her file on your claim is...bad. Because victims feel very vulnerable, adjusters often appear to be in a position of power and direction. This illusion of power can have extraordinary consequences on people who are unprepared, or to use clearer words, 'completely ignorant' about the disaster recovery process."[6]

The role of the adjuster is also to help protect the insurance company against fraudulent claims; if they think a claim is false, they become suspicious and will investigate.

The best thing you can do is to keep focused and open to learning so you don't fall in the "completely ignorant" category. Know what the adjuster's role is and understand your own.

One last thing about the adjuster – **do not** let your adjuster talk directly to your contractor. Tell your adjuster, "A contractor cannot negotiate my claim. If you have questions about my house, ask me and I will find out from my contractor." (California Insurance Code §2695.2c and §2695.5.)

(For more on this topic, see Chapter 8, "Insurance Company in Direct Contact with Your Contractor," on page 94.)

---

[6] Alford, Ron. *How to Win the Insurance Claims Game.* Plan Publishing Company, 1992.

Communicating to Protect Your Claim

One of our underlying goals is to help you finish your claim without the need for litigation. That being said, the better you prepare for litigation the less likely you are to need it. If you do happen to need litigation (and sometimes the decision is completely out of your control), the documentation you've created can make or break your case.

The insurance company has been preparing for litigation by keeping track of every phone call and correspondence you've had with them since the day you called for your first insurance quote (i.e., "this call is being monitored for *quality control* purposes"). The insurance company needs to see the side of you that is cool, calm, reasonable and organized. Your potential attorney will need to know your side of the story to decide if you have a case. The court needs to hear your side of the story to determine who to rule for. The documentation you create is your side of the story.

1. Keep a claim diary. A sample can be found on page 11.

    - If an agreement was made verbally or in writing, include the details of the agreement in your diary. Include copies of all correspondence.

    - Confirm in writing all information regarding coverage. Insist all insurance company responses be in writing.

2. When making phone calls, William Shernoff suggests to us in his insightful book *Payment Refused* to keep track of conversations in your diary and do the following:

> *Have all your papers – your policy, the claim form, related bills – close at hand when you make the telephone call. Save your telephone bills because a serious insurance problem may require long-distance telephone calls, and the phone bill will prove the call was made and the exact date you spoke to the company."*

> *Always ask for the identity of the person to whom you are speaking and whether he or she has the authority to handle your questions. Keep a telephone log of the dates, times and telephone numbers. Follow up your conversation with a brief letter to that person, summarizing your understanding of the substance of the call and ask him or her to respond by a certain date if your understanding is incorrect. Even if you are unable to obtain any information of substance, enter into your telephone log what transpired during the conversation.*[7]

> **TIP:** use your cell phone since all phone calls are tracked and reported on your monthly bill. Local and toll-free numbers won't show up on a landline phone bill. "

3. After a face-to-face meeting, note it in your diary and send a brief description of the conversation, including your conclusions, in writing to the adjuster and the main office.

4. Make sure all communication is in writing (fax, email or written letters). If the adjuster claims he is not receiving correspondence or if you have special correspondence, send it by certified mail *and* fax/email (to speed the company's response). Keep copies of any documentation or receipts that show it was sent.

5. Once again, Mr. Shernoff's advice for corresponding with the insurance company from his book *Payment Refused* comes in handy: *When you write to your insurance company, do the following:*

a) Explain your concern; always include your policy number.

---

[7] Shernoff, William. *Payment Refused*. William & Sons, 2004.

b) *Enclose copies of relevant information such as your claim forms and the bills or invoices for which you are claiming coverage.*

c) *Insist that the company make a written response to your inquiry, and give them a reasonable deadline for reply. (California Insurance Code §2695.5(b) says they should respond in no more than 15 calendar days after receipt of a claimant's communication.)*

d) *Keep a copy of all correspondence. Never send original material without keeping a copy for yourself.*[8]

Additional Letter Writing Tips

- Be diplomatic.

- Be brief –"fewer words, fewer problems."

- Avoid any threat of litigation in the wording of your communications; any hint of litigation tends to "tick off" the adjuster and may then lead to involvement by the insurance company's legal department. Provoking the insurance company's lawyers is probably the last thing you want to happen during the claim process.

> *TIP: Policies vary from year to year and from insurance company to insurance company. Get a complete copy from your company. Read and reread your own policy. Use a yellow highlighter to emphasize relevant sections of your policy.*

Key Policy Deadlines

Following a devastating catastrophic loss, insurance companies often waive the **60-day and 180-day deadlines**. We have found they rarely, if ever, waive the **one-year deadline to file a lawsuit** against them.

> *TIP: Depreciation is a negotiable issue.*

60 Day "Proof of Loss"

Policies have a provision which may require you to submit a notarized (signed and sworn) Proof of Loss within 60 days of your fire loss or 60 days after the claim representative requests it. Check and highlight your policy language.

The claim representative will usually provide you with a one- or two-page form. Be very careful with this form and do not ignore it. If the claim rep has already filled it out, the dollar amounts entered on the form can limit your actual loss recovery to the numbers they have provided.

Please see page 29 for more information on the Proof of Loss.

180-Day "Replacement" Provision

This policy provision may require you to replace your lost personal property and/or to rebuild or replace your damaged or lost house and other real property within 180 days of your loss, OR 180 days after the claim is settled OR 180 days after the Actual Cash Value of your property is paid. Again, check and highlight your insurance policy language.

Recent California insurance code changes extend the "Replacement" provision to one year (or 2 years in a declared emergency). Your policy may not show this revised requirement. To be certain, ask you agent or adjuster about this policy provision. To be safe, you may want to write your company to get their written reply about how they will handle this requirement.

> *TIP: Write your insurance claim representative to request a waiver or extension of the 180-day replacement requirements on both your dwelling (and other structures when necessary) and your personal property.*
>
> *(See sample 180-Day Replacement Letter on page 34.)*

---

[8] Shernoff, William. *Payment Refused*. William & Sons, 2004.

Your failure to comply with this policy provision allows your insurance company to **NOT PAY** you the amount of money the claim representative decided was the DEPRECIATION or hold back (see page 46 for a full definition) on your real and/or personal property. This can amount to tens of thousands of dollars!

This requirement may make sense if you have a small loss but when you have lost everything, 180 (or even 365 or 730) days to create a personal property inventory *and* replace all of the hundreds or thousands of personal property items on your list makes no sense whatsoever. Furthermore, the policy often requires you to replace or rebuild your damaged or destroyed house with the same time deadline.

In certain circumstances this deadline might be overridden by law, such as California Insurance Code §2051.5, which "Allows at least 12 months to rebuild and still receive replacement costs with possibility of a six-month extension. If a declared disaster (Governor's State of Emergency), homeowner/insured has at least 24 months to repair, rebuild or replace the home."[9]

If your claim representative refuses to waive or extend the "replacement" requirement deadline, call your state's Department of Insurance, talk to a consumer assistance organization, and/or get together with other survivors to see how they handled the situation.

180-Day Replacement Letter

Although some policies and current insurance code automatically extend the 180-day replacement provision to 12 or 24 months, you will still need to write a letter describing your intentions. This may preserve rights you may need down the road.

If you do not make a timely claim for replacement cost value you may lose your right to receive full replacement cost for items that have been paid on an actual cash value basis. In other words, you could lose your right to any depreciation that has been withheld on your dwelling or your personal property (see page 46 for examples of and information on depreciation).

Send this letter certified return, receipt requested or via FedEx or UPS.

[POLICY NUMBER]

[CLAIM NUMBER]

Dear [ADJUSTER/INSURANCE COMPANY NAME]:

Thank you for assisting us in returning to normal following our loss.

We are making claim for full replacement cost value under the [dwelling, other structures and/or personal property] coverage of our policy within 180 days [or one year] of our loss. Our loss occurred [DATE]. We intend to completely rebuild or replace our lost property.

Under the circumstances of a total loss such as ours, your requirement to rebuild or replace our dwelling [and other structures, if included] and our personal property is clearly impracticable and unreasonable. Please extend these policy requirements to at least two years. Please let us know, in writing, within 15 calendar days.

Thank you.

Sincerely,

[HOMEOWNER NAME & SIGNATURE]

---

[9] 8/20/10. description of laws can be found at
http://www.insurance.ca.gov/consumer-alerts/2007newlawsnoticecawildfire.cfm
or http://www.leginfo.ca.gov/cgi-bin/displaycode?section=ins&group=02001-03000&file=2050-2060

One-Year Rule to File a Lawsuit

Almost all California fire and homeowner insurance policies contain a provision that limits the time to file a lawsuit to one year following the date of the loss. We have never known an insurer to waive this deadline.

Although the one-year deadline is not always associated directly with the one-year anniversary of your loss (for more information see "How is the One-Year Deadline Calculated?" on page 35), it is a good benchmark to help assess where you are in the process. Mark your calendar at nine months after your loss to seriously review your insurance settlement situation.

> *TIP: Mark the NINTH MONTH date from your loss event on your calendar. You and your "bad faith" attorney will need time to prepare the appropriate legal documents.*

At the Nine-Month Anniversary

If you believe your insurance company under-insured you or treated you unfairly, improperly, or in "bad faith," you will need to review your circumstances with a qualified plaintiff's insurance attorney to see if you need to comply with the one-year deadline. A plaintiff's attorney who specializes in insurance law is the most qualified person to assess any benefits and remedies you may have under your insurance policy and the law.

Take the time to write a letter to your insurance company inquiring about the one-year deadline. Use the sample letter on page 36.

Do not wait until the last few weeks or days before complying with the one-year deadline! Attorneys will be busy with other survivors and may be less available to handle your sudden requirements. It takes time to adequately review your situation and prepare paperwork. Even if you find out you do not need to sue or meet the one-year deadline, give yourself enough time to fully protect your rights if you have legal issues regarding your insurance settlement. Give yourself at least that peace of mind. Five years from now you don't want to be stuck wondering "what would've happened if..." when it's well past the cut off.

Be aware that some insurance companies may try to delay in an effort to let the one-year deadline in your policy expire. Do not let this happen; make sure you understand all your options well before the deadline.

For more information, read "Attorneys and the Insurance Claim" on page 101.

You owe it to yourself to have your insurance recovery evaluated by a qualified legal professional and learn all of your options before the end of the one-year statute. Be fully informed before signing a release or making any final decisions!

At the 12-month anniversary

Not only will this be the date commemorating your slow but successful return to at least partial normalcy, it might be the last day you can file suit against your insurance company for any improper conduct or underpayment stemming from the settlement of your property insurance loss.

How is the One-Year Deadline Calculated?

There are three different ways by which one-year deadlines to file a lawsuit regarding a claim against your insurer are calculated:

- *Contract* – The insurance policy itself sets it at one year from the date of the loss.

- *Statute* – California Insurance Code §2071 (and §2070) maintains it is one year from the date the claim is fully paid, closed, or from the date a letter from the insurer saying it is closed issued.

- *Case law* – Prudential-LMI v Superior Court (delayed discovery rule) determined it is one year from discovery of the loss.

To avoid any unexpected complications, expense or dismissal, it is always safest and best to rely on the shortest deadline. One year from the exact day of the loss is the latest to file a timely lawsuit without incurring arguments from the insurance defense attorneys that the case be dismissed for an untimely filing.

Determine Your Deadline to File Suit Using This Sample Letter

[POLICY NUMBER]

[CLAIM NUMBER]

Dear [ADJUSTER/INSURANCE COMPANY NAME]:

Please advise in writing the exact date of our one-year deadline for filing suit.

Thank you for your immediate response.

Sincerely,

[HOMEOWNER SIGNATURE]

[HOMEOWNER NAME]

Chapter 4 **Understanding Your Policy**

Coverage Overview:

COVERAGES	Column 1 COVERAGE SET BY COMPANY Fill in the dollar amount from your policy	Column 2 % of Coverage A Each coverage is a percent of Coverage A. Calculate by dividing the dollar amount of each row in column 1 by the dwelling coverage amount in column 1	Column 3 COVERAGE SHOULD BE Fill in Coverage A from your Scope of Loss as the top number, then multiply by the % in column 2	Column 4 AMOUNT PAID TO DATE Fill in these numbers from the checks you have received
Coverage A: DWELLING				
Coverage A Extension				
Other				
Coverage A Subtotal		**A Subtotal:**		
Coverage B: OTHER STRUCTURES				
Other				
Coverage B Subtotal		**B Subtotal:**		
Coverage C: CONTENTS				
Scheduled Contents				
Other				
Coverage C Subtotal		**C Subtotal:**		
Coverage D: ADD'L LIVING EXP				
Other		or actual loss		
Coverage D Subtotal		**D Subtotal:**		
Other Coverages				
Debris removal - A				
Debris removal - B				
Debris removal - C				
Trees, plants, shrubs, lawns				
Building Code Upgrade				
Land Stabilization				
Other Coverages Subtotal		**OC Subtotal**		
TOTALS:				

An interactive spreadsheet complete with mathematical equations can be downloaded on our website. Look for "Confidential Loss Worksheet" in the insurance section of our Downloads Page at www.carehelp.org.

Tasks For This Chapter

☐   Determine what kind of policy you have.

☐   Determine your limits for AT LEAST the four major coverages and fill them into the chart on page 37.

☐   Understand ACV and RCV (see page 45).

☐   Read about Underinsurance on page 47.

What Kind of Policy Do You Have?

Once you get a copy of your policy you'll want to determine what type of coverage you have. Please note that Extended Replacement is the most common coverage sold. In California, the types of coverage offered by your insurance company are outlined in the "California Residential Property Insurance Disclosure" as mandated by California law. The following example was found online.[10]

One of the pages in your policy and/or renewal packet should look similar to the following:

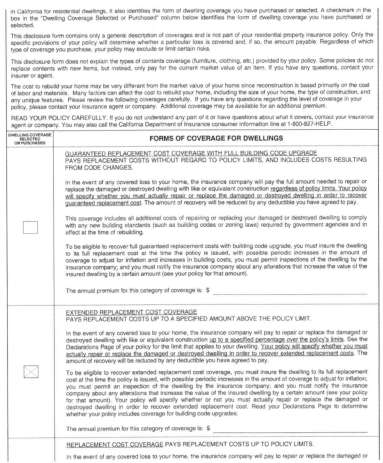

Figure 2: Insurance Policy Disclosure Form

Let's go over the text included on this form.

Guaranteed Replacement Cost Coverage

"In the event of any covered loss to your home, the insurance company will pay the full amount needed to repair or replace the damaged or destroyed dwelling with like or equivalent construction regardless of policy limits. Your policy will specify whether you must actually repair or replace the damaged or destroyed dwelling in order to recover guaranteed replacement cost. The amount of recovery will be reduced by any deductible you have agreed to pay."

This means that if the coverage amount shown on your declarations page is $100,000 for your dwelling, but it actually costs $175,000 to rebuild your identical house, they are obligated to pay the full $175,000.

---

[10] 9/16/2010. http://www.agencysoftware.com/download/pdf/67CA.pdf

Extended Replacement Cost Coverage

"In the event of any covered loss to your home, the insurance company will pay to repair or replace the damaged or destroyed dwelling with like or equivalent construction <u>up to a specified percentage over the policy's limits</u>. See the Declarations Page of your policy for the limit that applies to your dwelling. <u>Your policy will specify whether you must actually repair or replace the damaged or destroyed dwelling in order to recover extended replacement costs</u>. The amount of recovery will be reduced by any deductible you have agreed to pay."

Let's say the extension on your policy is 25 percent. If the coverage amount shown on your declarations page is $100,000 for your dwelling, but it actually costs $175,000 to rebuild your identical house, they are obligated to pay $100,000 plus 25 percent or $125,000.

Replacement Cost Coverage

"In the event of any covered loss to your home, the insurance company will pay to repair or replace the damaged or destroyed dwelling with like or equivalent construction <u>up to the policy's limits</u>. See the Declarations Page of your policy for the limit that applies to your dwelling. <u>Your policy will specify whether you must actually repair or replace the damaged or destroyed dwelling in order to recover this benefit</u>. The amount of recovery will be reduced by any deductible you have agreed to pay. To be eligible to recover this benefit, you must insure the dwelling to 100 percent."

This means that if the coverage amount shown on your declarations page is $100,000 for your dwelling, but it actually costs $175,000 to rebuild your identical house, they are only obligated to pay the limit of $100,000.

Actual Cash Value Coverage

"In the event of any covered loss to your home, the insurance company will pay either the fair market value of the damaged or destroyed dwelling (excluding the value of the land) at the time of the loss, or the cost of replacing or repairing the damaged or destroyed dwelling with like or equivalent construction <u>up to the policy limit, with possible consideration of physical depreciation</u>. The amount of recovery will be reduced by any deductible you have agreed to pay."

This means that if the coverage amount shown on your declarations page is $100,000 for your dwelling, but it actually costs $175,000 to rebuild your house, a few things have to be calculated before a payout amount is determined.

First it must be determined how much the house has depreciated. (See page 46 to learn more about depreciation and page 64 for a list of things that are and are not depreciable in your dwelling.) If the depreciated cost or fair market value of the house is determined to be $50,000 then they are only obligated to pay $50,000.

If it was determined that the value of the house had depreciated $50,000, then that portion is subtracted from the actual cost of repair. In this example, $175,000 minus $50,000 leaves $125,000. But since your limit is only $100,000, they are only obligated to pay $100,000.

If, on the other hand, your limit is $100,000 and the actual cost to rebuild the house is $125,000 – and it is determined that the depreciated cost of the house is $90,000 – then the amount the insurance company is obligated to pay is $90,000.

Fortunately, very few policies in California are ACV policies.

Building Code Upgrade – Ordinance or Law Coverage

"In the event of any covered loss, the insurance company will pay any additional costs, up to the stated limits, of repairing or replacing a damaged or destroyed dwelling to conform to any building standards such as building codes or zoning laws required by government agencies and in effect at the time of the loss or rebuilding."

If you have this coverage, it can cover portions of your repair that you didn't necessarily have prior to the loss, but that your municipality now requires through upgrades to the building codes due to new ordinances or laws enacted after your house was built.

This means that given this scenario:

- the coverage amount shown on your declarations page is $100,000 for the dwelling

- an additional 10 percent[11] is provided for building code upgrades

- the actual cost to rebuild the house is $175,000, and

- the portion of the rebuild determined to be required by law is $20,000

Then the amount the insurance company owes you is as follows:

> $100,000 stated limit
>
> $ 25,000 extension (if you have Extended Replacement coverage at 25 percent)
>
> $ 10,000 building code upgrade limit (based on 10 percent coverage found in many policies)
>
> $135,000 total (or $110,000 if you have no extension)

> **TIP**: *Building Code Upgrade coverage can sometimes be called Ordinance or Law which is sometimes abbreviated to "OL".*

Depending on the policy language, the Building Code Upgrade percentage should also apply to the replacement extension percentage of Coverage A. If this is the case, the example above would include an additional amount of coverage as follows:

> $100,000 stated limit
>
> $ 25,000 extension (if you have Extended Replacement coverage at 25 percent)
>
> $ 10,000 building code upgrade limit (10 percent of $100,000 stated limit)
>
> $ 2,500 building code upgrade limit (10 percent of $25,000 extension)
>
> $137,500 total

Sometimes Building Code Upgrade coverage is built into the Dwelling coverage, which means it does not increase the dollar amount beyond your existing Dwelling coverage. Read your policy to see which you have.

> $100,000 stated limit
>
> $ 10,000 building code upgrade limit (only applies if damage is less than $100,000)
>
> $100,000 total (total coverage is always $100,000)

In the above example, if the policyholder had $100,000 in dwelling coverage and 10 percent Building Code Upgrade coverage *built into* the policy limits, and they suffered a $50,000 loss, they would have an additional $10,000 available to cover items required due to new building codes. If on the other hand the loss was $100,000 or more, no additional monies would be available.

For more detail on Building Code Upgrade coverage, please see page 84.

---

[11] Some policy endorsements can change the percentage for Building Code Upgrade, which we have seen range from 5% to 50%, and even 100%.

Declarations Page

Once you've determined the kind of policy you purchased, you'll want to take a look at the **Declarations Page.** Here, we will try to demystify it for you.

The Declarations Page or **"Dec Page"** is usually a one- or two-page notice you received in the mail shortly after you initially got your homeowners policy. Each year you receive a new Dec Page with that year's stated limits. Some policies have the same limits each year, but many limits change from year to year. The Dec Page states the dollar limits of all your coverages (see Section 2 in sample below) as set by the insurance company and contains a *list* of all endorsements and all other documents required (Section 3 in sample below) by your state that changes or modifies your initial insurance contract or policy.

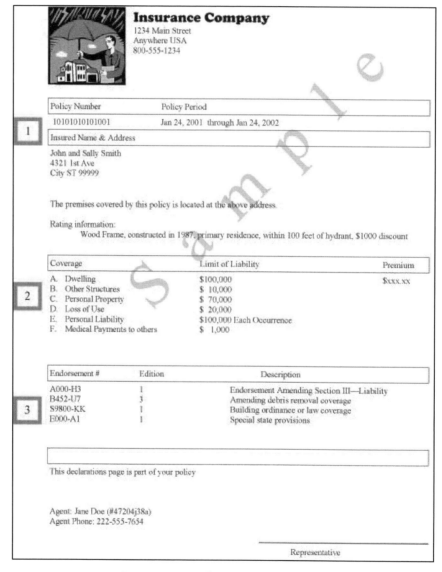

Figure 3: Sample Declarations Page
(boxed numbers on left are for reference only)

Besides the policy itself, the Dec Page (or a computer printout similar to the Dec Page) is usually the starting point for the insurance adjuster to determine the basic *value* of your loss. With the Dec Page (or a similar document sometimes provided by your agent or insurance company after a loss) in his or her hands, the adjuster will usually begin to determine your settlement. We have heard some homeowners report that the adjuster looked for several moments at the debris or damage, then at the Dec Page, and said: "Well, you've certainly exceeded your limits." They then wrote a check for the Dwelling limits (Coverage A) and left.

Most adjusters, though, begin by saying he or she will begin the process of determining your loss (or adjusting your loss) and start the paperwork by asking you questions about your dwelling.

You might ask, "Why should we hire a qualified expert to determine the scope of the loss when the insurance company says it will figure that out?" A better question is why are they so determined to do this tedious job when they are not obligated to do so under the policy and are probably overworked by all their other claims? (Determining the amount of your loss is one of **your** duties listed in the policy section "Duties after loss.")

> *The dwelling coverage is your most important insurance coverage; it is the dollar amount upon which all of the rest of your coverages are based.*

The answer to this question is the key to your entire claims process. The dwelling coverage is your most important insurance coverage; it is the dollar amount upon which all of the rest of your coverages are based. If the insurance adjustor – not you, the homeowner – controls the process by which the dwelling loss portion of your settlement is determined, then it is the adjuster who is in control of your entire claim amount. (See "The Relationship Between the Coverages" on page 44.) This is to be avoided.

The Different Coverages in Your Policy

Here is a non-exhaustive list of the coverages in a standard policy and a short explanation of each. See your own policy for the coverages you have and more detailed definitions.

Dwelling Coverage

(Usually Coverage A)

The insurance company insured your house as it stood **before** the loss. Most policies include language that states they will pay for "*like kind and quality*" when replacing the house you lost. This means if the dwelling had plaster walls, single paned aluminum windows and hardwood floors, they should pay for the cost of these "like" items, without regard for what materials you plan to use in your new house.

Other Structures Coverage

(Usually Coverage B but some, like State Farm, include it in A)

Your **Other Structures** clause may read: "We will cover other structures on the residence premises, **separated** *from the dwelling by clear space.* Other Structure coverage includes structures connected to the dwelling by **only** *a fence, utility line or similar connection.*" (See page 83 for more details.)

Personal Property Coverage

(Usually Coverage C but some, like State Farm for example, call it Coverage B)

This includes items that you would normally take with you when you move. Don't leave out small items such as Band-Aids, toothpicks and hangers. These small items can add up to thousands of dollars when you try to replace them. Potted plants can also be included here. See Chapter 6 for help with documenting this loss.

Additional Living Expenses (ALE or Loss of Use)

(Usually Coverage D)

Some frequently forgotten examples are:

- Additional automobile expenses (including fuel) for additional miles you drive due to relocation.
- Hookup fees for utilities at your temporary location.
- Laundry bills above your normal costs.
- Costs of replacing certificates and diplomas.
- Supplies specific to an RV, such as toilet chemicals.
- Electrical bills above what was previously paid (most electric companies charge more per kWh for electricity served through a temporary pole).

(See page 79 for additional information.)

Other Coverages

See Chapter 7, "Other Coverages" on page 86 for other coverages that might be available to you.

The Relationship Between the Coverages

Most of the coverages are based on a percentage of the Dwelling Coverage. Generally, when you add the dwelling coverage together with all your other coverages the total is *at least double* your dwelling coverage amount, as in the following example (percentages will vary by policy). Please see the corresponding chapters for more information on each of the coverages listed below.

Example One:

Dwelling		$100,000
Other Structures	10%*	10,000
Personal Property	50%	50,000
ALE	30%	30,000
Landscaping	5%	5,000
Debris Removal	5%	5,000
Total		**$200,000**

Example Two:

Dwelling		$200,000
Other Structures	10%	20,000
Personal Property	50%	100,000
ALE	30%	60,000
Landscaping	5%	10,000
Debris Removal	5%	10,000
Total		**$400,000**

*The percentages indicate a percentage of the dwelling coverage amount.

The result of this is if the dwelling portion of the policy is estimated incorrectly, it can negatively impact your recovery if you're underinsured (see page 47 for more information on Underinsurance).

RCV, ACV and Depreciation Defined

Application and definition of the insurance terms **Replacement Cost Value** (RCV), **Actual Cash Value** (ACV) and **depreciation** can be confusing. It's important that you understand the terms to help settle your claim fairly.

An easy way to understand RCV and ACV is to think in terms of "new" and "used." Replacement cost is the item's *current price, new*. "What will it cost when I replace it?" Actual cash is the item's *used price, old*. "How much money is it worth since I used it for five years?"

Hold Back

Most policies only pay the Actual Cash Value upfront, and then they pay you the "held back" depreciation after you incur the expense to repair or replace your personal property items.

NOTE: You must remember to send documentation to the insurance company proving you've incurred the additional expense you will be reimbursed.

Replacement Cost (RCV)

Replacement Cost is based on replacing the lost or damaged building material or personal property item with an exact replacement equal to the original. If the building material or personal property item is no longer available, the replacement may possibly be better than the original.

Replacement Cost Value (RCV) is the maximum amount your insurance company will pay you for damage to covered property *before deducting for depreciation*. The RCV payment is based on the *current cost* to replace your property with new, identical or comparable property.

Example: Five years ago you paid $100 plus sales tax for an item. The item is no longer available, but a comparable item currently costs $125 plus sales tax. With RCV coverage, the maximum amount your insurance company will pay you for the item is $125 plus sales tax.

> *TIP*: Do not rely on your insurance claims adjuster to set RCV, ACV or depreciation values for your real or personal property. Educate yourself or find qualified professionals to protect your interests. It will save you time and will be money well spent.

Actual Cash Value (ACV)

Actual Cash Value (ACV) is the amount your insurance company will pay you for damage to covered property *after deducting for depreciation*. ACV is the replacement cost of a new item, minus depreciation. If stated as a simple equation, ACV could be defined as follows: ACV=RCV-Depreciation

Example: Five years ago you paid $100 plus sales tax for an item. Since ACV is the current replacement cost less depreciation, you must consider "wear and tear," if any. If the item had a reasonable life expectancy of ten years, and you used it for five years, the item possibly could have lost 50 percent of its value. The item, or an equivalent if the item is no longer available, currently costs $125. With ACV coverage, the maximum amount your insurer will pay you for the item is $62.50 (current replacement cost is $125, minus 50 percent depreciation).

Unfortunately, ACV is not always as easy to agree upon as a simple math equation. The ACV can also be calculated as the price a willing buyer would pay for your used item.

> *TIP*: Although time consuming, negotiate ACV and depreciation on an item-by-item basis to reflect your specific usage and the real "wear and tear" on the item. Items with no wear and tear may have 100% of their value.

Depreciation

Depreciation (sometimes called "hold back") is defined as the "loss in value from all causes, including age, and wear and tear." Although the definition seems to be clear, in our experience, "value" as a real-world application is clearly subjective and varies widely. We have seen the same adjuster apply NO depreciation (100 percent value) on one claim and 40 percent depreciation (almost half value) on an almost identical claim. This shows that the process of applying depreciation is subjective and clearly negotiable.

Although insurers generally rely on "in-house" computer generated depreciation schedules or even the IRS depreciation schedule, depreciation should always be _negotiated_ with your adjuster. No one, and certainly not the IRS or an insurance company's computer software, is better equipped to assess the actual condition of your personal property than you are.

Since value is a subjective measure, depreciation is always negotiable! Adjusters will try to convince you otherwise. If they do convince you, the negotiations are over. They write in the file, "Homeowner agreed."

Example: You own two identical sofas. One sofa is in your "sitting" room and has rarely been used. The other sofa is located in the family room and has been used extensively. Depreciation will be different for each sofa. _Negotiate any depreciation_! (See page 74 for "Depreciation on Personal Property Items." See page 64 for "What is Depreciable in the Dwelling Coverage.")

Although determining the ACV is stated as one of "Your Duties After a Loss," (see page 72, Figure 10 for policy examples) the insurance company will usually determine depreciation for your claim even if you include an estimated ACV in your inventory. Be aware that any depreciation they calculate is arbitrary. You can negotiate depreciation.

Excessive Depreciation

When the insurance company depreciates more than they should, it is called "Excessive Depreciation." Although not ethical, it is very common. Note any items that have excessive depreciation and write a letter to your insurance company.

NOTE: Some insurance companies will try to depreciate an item the adjuster believes you will never replace by as much as 90 percent. We have seen adjusters try to depreciate books by that high a percentage. They reason you will never read it again, but what book read only once is no longer of any real value? Negotiate for full value.

What is Underinsurance?

Underinsurance is when you don't have enough insurance to cover your loss. Underinsurance is a legal issue as it is something that is extra-contractual, meaning it is not something mentioned in your policy so legal council will always be used by an insurance company when this issue is brought to their attention.

Within days, if not hours, following a wildfire adjusters, some agents and insurance contractors inform already dazed fire victims that they are underinsured. Usually, this is the first time the homeowner has even considered that their coverage might not be adequate.

Over the years we've talked to thousands of people who have lost their homes to natural disasters. We have found that over 90 percent of the people we talk to not only are underinsured, but are *grossly* underinsured.

> *"...over 90 percent of the people we talk to not only are underinsured, but are* **grossly** *underinsured."*

Through interviews, we've found that only 8 percent of the people we've talked to who lost their houses in the 2007 wildfires were insured to at least 80 percent of their loss. Only 2 percent were insured to 90 percent of their loss. On average, the majority of the dwellings were only covered for 55 percent of their replacement value.

Even though insurance companies might claim to not be the expert in property valuation (a common claim they make when discussing the issue in public) they have the ability to determine exact dwelling coverage amounts using sophisticated and costly computer programs which they already own. To prove the accuracy of their software, one provider called Marshall & Swift, claimed in a June 18, 2003 press release "...more than 70 years of experience [with] over 100,000 individual users, including underwriters, claims adjusters, inspectors, and agents."[12]

Furthermore, even though insurance companies knew that reconstruction costs exceeded $200/square foot after the 2003 wildfires, 85 percent of the people we interviewed who suffered losses in 2007 were insured at less than $200/square foot.

How Did I Become Underinsured?

When you call to buy your policy, companies typically use a construction cost and dwelling evaluation computer program like Marshall & Swift's "Residential Component Technology." The computer programs are sophisticated and have been "perfected" over many years.

If ALL parameters are input, an accurate replacement cost (Coverage A limit) for your dwelling can easily be determined. This process usually takes about 15 minutes, but unfortunately the agents can use built-in shortcuts which can lead to underestimating the rebuild value.

These are the minimum required fields in the software to determine a coverage amount:

- Zip Code
- Building Type (Related to occupancy)
- Stories/levels
- Square Footage
- Construction Type

---

[12] 04/04/11. http://www.trainingpressreleases.com/newsstory.asp?NewsID=680

Do these questions sound familiar? When you've called an insurance agency or company to get a quote, are these the questions they've asked? It's possible they used only the minimum required fields to determine the rebuild value of your house which resulted in underinsurance.

Why do Companies Underinsure?

It's hard to imagine why insurance companies would give up additional premiums by underinsuring customers, but we find they do it every day. Why?

- **Most losses (99 percent) are small, partial losses, so why insure for the 1 percent of total losses?**

- **To compete in the marketplace.**

  Everyone else does it and no one wants to be the first to charge more.

- **To keep their good neighborly hands on your annual premium payment.**

  If they raise your premium, you're likely to shop elsewhere.

- **To limit their overall exposure and risk.**

  The premium collected for the increase in coverage might not be worth the small increase in income. Selling this coverage to everyone would increase the amount of exposure to the company without the same degree of increase in premium.

- **To shift the risk to the homeowner.**

  If they don't sell that additional coverage, they don't have to pay you that additional amount if you are the 1 percent with a total loss.

- **To reduce their re-insurance expenses.**

  If they sell you more coverage, they have to buy more re-insurance coverage. (Re-insurance is the insurance the insurance company's buy to help cover costs when they have to pay claims. Yes, they insure insurance.)

It's Not Your Fault!

The bottom line here is that being underinsured is not your fault. Expert insurance consumer attorneys Jerry Ramsey and Brian Heffernan ask you to consider what happened when you purchased your insurance:

> "When is the last time that anyone walked into their agent's office to purchase homeowners insurance and was asked 'Well how much would you like?'[13]

In most cases, the insurance company determined the amount of the dwelling coverage. They are the experts on insurance coverage. They have access to ALL construction cost databases. They use computer programs to play with your coverage amount – and "confirm" it by preparing documents that show a low damage repair amount once you have an insured loss.

Is There a Remedy to Underinsurance After a Loss?

Yes. It's called negotiation. Usually negotiation to settle beyond policy limits takes place after an attorney is hired by the homeowner. In some situations, however, insurance companies are willing to negotiate above policy limits without involving an attorney.

---

[13] Ramsey & Heffernan, "UNDERINSURANCE, A Consumer Fraud, Not an Agent Error of Omission." *Forum.* June 2004.

In any negotiation process, you will not be able to properly negotiate without first documenting your loss. Do not short change yourself by declaring yourself underinsured and prematurely getting into a negotiation without having proper documentation.

Before You Report Underinsurance

When you report an underinsurance issue to your insurance company they are required by insurance regulations to investigate. This means they'll forward your claim to their legal department or other special investigative department (sometimes called SHU or "Special Handling Unit") which could delay handling of your claim.

Before you report an underinsurance issue to them you should do the following:

- Get paid up to your policy limits, or as much as they're willing to pay (see Chapter 8 "Negotiating with your Insurance Adjuster").

- Document your entire loss with hard estimates including a Scope of Loss and your personal property inventory (use the chart at the beginning of this chapter).

- Develop a list of specific instances where you think they acted in bad faith.

- Make sure you have a claim diary, or start one now. (See page 11.)

- Interview potential attorneys for your case. (See Chapter 9 for information on hiring a professional.)

When the Adjuster's Actions Conflict with the Policy

So you've read this whole chapter, but your understanding of the policy is still different than the adjusters. Here are some common conflicts you might run into.

You're Asked to Do Things That Aren't Required By the Policy

This might include signing paperwork or filling out long and arduous forms. You can ask the adjuster to identify these requirements in the policy. When they offer a response, ask for it in writing so you can study it later or record it in your notes and, if necessary, tell the adjuster you'll get back to them. Ask any follow-up questions in writing.

See also see Chapter 8 "Negotiating with your Insurance Adjuster".

Conflicting Understanding of the Policy

Your understanding of your policy may very well not gibe with what you're hearing from your adjuster. Don't be discouraged from communicating your view on any point of contention. You might even want to express your opinion in writing. Silence will be understood as consent; they will assume you've changed your mind and now agree with the adjuster's perspective.

In the end, the reasonable interpretation of the policy should be more favorable to the insured than the insurance company. The following was extracted from a 2008 case that might help you understand how policy interpretation conflicts are hashed out in court:[14]

> *In California, the interpretation of an insurance policy follows a well-established set of rules. As a general matter, "the mutual intention of the parties at the time the contract is formed governs [contract] interpretation." To discern the mutual intent of the parties, a court should apply the following rules, in sequence.*
>
> Rule 1: The Plain Meaning. *If possible, the mutual intent of the parties is to be "inferred...solely from the written provisions of the contract."*
>
> Rule 2: The Insured's Objectively Reasonable Expectations. *If a provision has no "clear and explicit meaning," ambiguity is "resolved by interpreting the ambiguous provisions in the sense the insurer believed the insured understood them at the time of formation."*
>
> Rule 3: The Contra-Insurer Rule. *If application of the first two rules still does not eliminate the ambiguity, "ambiguous language is construed against the party who caused the uncertainty to exist." At this stage, "any ambiguous terms are resolved in the insured's favor, consistent with the insured's reasonable expectations."*
>
> Rule 4: Exclusions Must be Conspicuous, Plain and Clear. *The law requires that an exclusionary clause in an insurance policy be conspicuous, plain and clear. This is especially true when the coverage portion of the policy would lead an insured to "reasonably expect coverage" for the claim purportedly excluded.*

---

[14] 8/21/11. http://ca.findacase.com/research/wfrmDocViewer.aspx/xq/fac.20080930_0013695.ECA.htm/qx

Chapter 5 **Dwelling Coverage**

Scope of Loss Check List

This is a list of things that will help you determine the quality of materials with which your pre-loss house was constructed, and how much it will cost to reconstruct with like-kind-and-quality materials. Please note that you will need more detail than is listed here to create a full Scope of Loss, but this will get you started on understanding what you need to think about and areas to research.

Floor plan of your house

If you've recently had work done on your house, the architect who designed the renovations or the contractor who had the permit pulled might still have a copy of your floor plan. If you're in a tract house: a) the municipality which permitted your house might keep a copy on file; b) someone in your neighborhood who has the same floor plan might have a copy if *they* recently had plans drawn for renovations; or c) the original builder might have the plans. Other resources include:

☐ An appraisal completed during purchase or refinance.
☐ Property tax documents.
☐ DIY – Do It Yourself (see page 56). If you live in a tract home, ask a neighbor with the same floor plan whose house didn't burn to allow you take measurements.

Plot plan of your property

☐ Assessor's Parcel Map from the county.
☐ Satellite photos (available on the internet).

Interior and exterior details of your house

☐ Your own photos or photos your friends, family or neighbors have of your house.
☐ In a housing tract, a neighbor's house with the same floor plan that remained standing can be invaluable. Take pictures of that house's common details, and especially those things usually hidden (inside of walls, etc.). Take A LOT of pictures before they repair and close things up.
☐ Your homeowner's association may be able to provide you with a list of any architectural details it requires

Construction details of your house. Describe the following:

1. One story / two story / split level (circle one)

2. Garage size: one-car / two-car / three-car / other: _____ (circle one)

3. Garage: attached / detached / carport / other (circle one)

4. Foundation: raised (crawlspace) / concrete / hillside (circle all that are applicable)

5. Roofing and roof drains: _____

6. Water, sewer, gas (evidence in rubble): copper / some type of plastic / steel (may be black) / septic

7. Location of utility panels, mains and/or meters: _____

8. Type of heating and air conditioning used: _____

9. Fireplaces? Y / N. How many and what kind: _____

10. Windows (number and type): _____

11. Garage door (number of doors and type, including door opener): _____

12. Exterior/entrance doors (number and type): _____

13. Interior doors (number and type): _____

Describe your kitchen:

1. Cabinets: _____

2. Countertops/backsplash: _____

3. Appliances/plumbing fixtures/trim (faucets and handles): _____

4. Flooring: _____

5. Wall covering: _____

6. Special ceiling conditions (include height): _____

7. No. of outlets, switches, light fixtures, ceiling fans and smoke detectors:_____

Describe your bathroom(s):

1. Cabinets: _____

2. Countertops/backsplash: _____

3. Plumbing fixtures (including tub/shower)/trim (faucets and handles): _____

4. Hardware (towel bars, etc.): _____

5. Flooring: _____

6. Wall covering: _____

7. Special ceiling conditions (include height): _____

8. No. of outlets, switches, light fixtures, ceiling fans and smoke detectors:_____

Describe your living/family room(s):

1. Built-in cabinets/countertops: _____

2. Flooring: _____

3. Wall covering: _____

4. Special ceiling conditions (include height): _____

5. Number of outlets, switches, light fixtures, ceiling fans and smoke detectors:_____

Describe your bedroom(s):

1. Built-in cabinets/countertops: _____

2. Flooring: _____

3. Wall covering: _____

4. Special ceiling conditions (include height): _____

5. No. of outlets, switches, light fixtures, ceiling fans and smoke detectors:_____

Describe common areas (halls, entry's etc.):

1. Flooring / wall covering: _____

2. Special ceiling conditions (include height): _____

3. No. of outlets, switches, light fixtures, ceiling fans and smoke detectors:_____

Tasks For This Chapter

☐   Decide who will complete your Scope of Loss and start the process.

☐   Collect information about the construction of the house that was destroyed. Use the checklist on page 51.

☐   Get a copy of the insurance company's Scope of Loss.

☐   Review the insurance company's Scope for inaccuracies and inappropriate use of depreciation. (Page 46 and 64.)

Determine Amount of Repair/Reconstruction

One of the most difficult insurance concepts for survivors is how the "replacement coverage" policy works. Most replacement coverage policies require the insurance company to pay you based on how much it would cost to "replace" the house you lost with "like-kind-and-quality" materials (see page 61 for more information on "like-kind-and-quality"). They insured the house you lost; they should *not* pay you based on the house you *will be building*. That new house, as we have found following a disaster, almost always will be different than the house that was damaged or lost, based on building code changes alone.

> "It is always more expensive to rebuild a home after a loss as compared to building a similar new home not associated with a claim."
>
> – Craig Locante for the Insurance Journal

It is important that you keep these two projects separate in your mind. The first project is to recreate the damaged or destroyed house on paper, and the second project is to complete the house rebuild or repairs.

What does this mean? The house needs to be reconstructed on paper in order to know the dollar amount of your loss. Once a dollar amount has been agreed upon, you will be able to create a budget so you can move forward with your project. Moving forward *without* a budget can prove disastrous.

After a disaster, many people will talk to a friend or other acquaintance who is a contractor or who recently did a construction project, about how much it costs per square foot to build a house. They get an estimate or "WAG" (wild absurd guess) figure and decide that this arbitrary number is suitable as an insurance settlement. Once you do your homework though, you may be surprised how much more it costs to "reconstruct" your house than it is to buy or even build a new home, especially if you were in a tract home.

Replacement Cost Estimation software expert Craig Locante has this to say about replacement cost and reconstruction vs. new construction:

> *"It is always more expensive to rebuild a home after a loss as compared to building a similar new home not associated with a claim. The biggest reason is economies of scale, but many other factors also contribute."* [15]

Why does it cost more to reconstruct an old home? According to The Rapid Survey Group[16]:

> *Older homes, generally those built before 1945, can cost up to 25 percent-45 percent more than a newer home to rebuild 'as-is'. Many features found in homes built before 1945** are more expensive to replicate and replace. Some 'old home' features that can contribute to an increase in replacement cost are:*
>
> o *Solid Wood Doors*
>
> o *Lath & Plaster Walls & Ceilings*
>
> o *Extensive Hardwood Flooring*
>
> o *Old Home Architectural Techniques*
>
> o *Custom Millwork*

---

[15] Locante, Craig. "Are You Stuck with Your Head in the Sand?" *The Insurance Journal*. Sept 6, 2004.

[16] *FAQ*. 2003. Rapid Survey Group. 1/13/2011. http://www.rapidsurveygroup.com/faqs.htm#horeplacementcost

** We have found that many of these features exist even in homes built after 1945. In fact, many homes built through the '50s and some into the 60s have plaster walls and ceilings. Many houses today are still constructed with solid hardwood floors.

- o *Antique Carving*
- o *Leaded Glass*
- o *Plaster Moldings*
- o *Antique Light Features*
- o *Quantity and Complexity of Moldings*

Some additional factors that can increase the cost to replace to "like kind and quality" are:

- Distance from construction suppliers and workers
- Congested roads, as a damaged area rebuilds all at the same time
- Security and protection of your property while the house is being repaired or rebuilt
- Irregular shape of the house – with many corners and turns on the exterior
- Irregular shape and slope of the roof – with hips and valleys
- Several different kinds of floor, wall and ceiling surfaces – a combination of tile, carpet, wood, or wallpaper, tile, paneling and paint
- Irregular shape of rooms and ceilings
- Ceilings measuring less than, or greater than, 8 feet
- Brick or stone fireplace
- A lot of glass or skylights
- Raised foundations

As you can see, there is a lot involved with determining your loss. In order to document it properly you will need to have a professional contractor help you create a Scope of Loss. Don't rush yourself. Your settlement will be more accurate and fair if you take the time to get the facts about your home construction straight.

What is a Scope of Loss

A **Scope of Loss** is similar to the personal property inventory. Like that document, the Scope of Loss is a detailed itemization of the quantity and quality of every component of your lost home. However, the Scope of Loss will also include all the construction costs necessary to repair or rebuild your lost home.

After your insurance contract (policy) and your insurance Declarations Page, the Scope of Loss is probably the most important document you will need to receive a fair and full settlement following an insured loss.

The Insurance Company's Scope of Loss

> *"...the Scope of Loss is a detailed itemization of the quantity and quality of every component of your lost home."*

The insurance company will send a representative to assess the damage done to your insured property. Sometimes they rely solely on the adjuster, but other times they send a contractor. The contractor is not necessarily there to actually perform the repairs, but they will often try to sell you their services. Think of the person sent by the insurance company as its representative to assess damages and to determine how much it wants to pay on your claim.

DO let them inspect the damage, answer all of their relevant questions, and work with them to create the most complete documentation possible.

Do NOT use this or any insurance company-recommended contractor. Their relationship to the insurance company is not in *YOUR* best interest.

We find that Scopes of Loss vary greatly. Some adjusters will give a very detailed Scope of Loss, while others (and sometimes from the same insurance company) give a very flimsy two- or three-page Scope of Loss, filled with only general construction categories. Some provide only a construction "estimate."

Developing Your Own Scope of Loss

To have ANY chance of attaining FULL coverage under your insurance policy, YOU must first determine exactly all of the features of the home you lost. After that, you'll need to hire a contractor to determine what it would cost TODAY to replace precisely what you had. You may be more interested in plans for what you hope to build, but it will be important right now to first focus on what you lost. Remember, your goal is to document and place a value on your actual loss.

Because most general contractors are not familiar with the Scope of Loss process, you may need a specialist. A Scope of Loss represents the total cost, including "hard costs" (labor and materials), "soft costs" (fees supervision, etc.), and overhead and profit, to replicate your lost home. It is not an estimated cost per square foot.

Having a contractor representing YOU through the Scope of Loss process is of utmost importance to make sure they catch everything. Just think of it as a second set of eyes. All works of importance (books, building plans, etc.) have some sort of stop-gap measure to verify the integrity of the work. This might be the most expensive and most important work you will complete. Don't shortchange yourself.

To find a professional to complete your Scope of Loss, look for references from "bad faith" or construction defect attorneys who represent homeowners.

We cannot emphasize enough the importance of a complete and accurate evaluation of the replacement cost of the house you lost. Remember: all other coverages, such as personal property, are usually directly linked to the dwelling cost (see Chapter 4, "The Relationship Between the Coverages" on page 44). An accurate Scope of Loss is extremely important as it documents any underinsurance issues you may have.

To create an accurate Scope of Loss, information is gathered from numerous sources. Please see the introductory check list for this chapter to start gathering information for a Scope of Loss.

General Conditions

Beyond the quality and quantity of materials listed in your Scope of Loss that you will document on the introductory tab, there are other expenses that will be incurred when rebuilding. **General Conditions** (also called **General Requirements** or a similar term) is the category in the Scope of Loss for the cost of items which are necessary for the repair of damages or reconstruction of a house but which are not the direct costs of materials and labor to rebuild the house. Items listed under General Conditions items do not become a physical part of the house but are all the expenses associated with the *intangible costs* of repairing or rebuilding the particular house at the particular site. **General Conditions can add 30 percent or more to the Scope of Loss beyond the expense of materials, labor, taxes and permits.**

> *"General conditions [are costs] which are necessary for the repair of damages or reconstruction of a house but which are not the direct costs of materials and labor to rebuild the house."*

The cost of General Conditions are different from, and are not a part of, contractor overhead and profit which are calculated after all actual construction items are finalized in the Scope of Loss. **Profit** is the surplus cost required to generate the incentive and mechanism necessary to keep the company a viable enduring company. Profit is the General Contractor's economic return for having invested his or her time and money in a risky, difficult and liability-ridden private enterprise. **Overhead,** on the other hand, pays for the office expenses – supplies, rent, utilities, secretarial and accounting staff, among other day to day costs.

Finally, if the insurance company claims representative and/or contractor tells you that your contractor's time or cost estimates are excessive, ask them to prove that their costs include *all* costs associated with the AIA and CSI construction "Division I"[17]. The general contractor must anticipate these cost increases or document the increases to the best of his or her ability.

Examples of General Conditions:

Most, if not all of the items listed below should be included in any major residential disaster repair or reconstruction project, plus specific LOCAL conditions which might include:

- Lower productivity of workers at due to site specific conditions – upslope or downslope
- Work congestion (300+/- structures built in two years instead of several decades)
- Main highway delays
- Local roadway detours and delays
- Narrow roads
- Weather delays
- Steep uphill or downhill sloped work sites
- Limited work and material storage areas
- Potential labor shortages
- Limited laborer facilities
- Increased delivery fees for materials and appliances

---

[17] For an overview, see the following: 08/24/11.
http://www.cdcr.ca.gov/CSA/FSO/Programs/2002ConstructionAuditGuide6thEd/docs/CSI_Divisions.html

Temporary Facilities

The following items might be required during the construction of a residence

- Porta-potty
- Temporary power pole
- Temporary power hookup (and fees)
- Electricity (for running power tools)
- Temporary water service
- Site fencing
- Security
- Temporary site lighting
- Temporary storage
- Dumpsters
- Continual cleanup
- Scaffolding
- Construction crane
- Consumable tools, protective coverings and safety equipment (for example, saw blades, coverings, goggles, raingear, first aid supplies)

Office Equipment

The following expenses may need to be considered in your Scope of Loss:

- Fax machine and supplies
- Plan reproduction
- Site office/trailer

Management and Supervision

OSHA regulations and standard AIA contracts require a full-time on-site supervisor. The supervisor is an employee of the general contractor. Some of the time, the supervisor is helping to repair or build the house, but most of the time he or she is supervising construction, coordinating subcontractors, ensuring that the job site is safe and other essential functions. In addition, the general contractor may need to budget a project manager to work part time on the project assisting the supervisor and making occasional visits to the job site. An architect's oversight is separate from these employees, but there may be some duplication of duties with the architect.

- Project Supervisor
- Project Manager

Contract Close-out

At the end of the job, the house is cleaned prior to the owner's re-occupation. At this time, the architect, inspector and/or the homeowner go through the house and prepare a "punch list" of tasks the general contractor must finish and/or redo before the project is signed off as complete and the general contractor can receive final payment.

- Final cleanup
- Final punch list (To fix dings, mistakes, paint touch-up, etc.)

Performance Bond

At 3%+/- of the total price of the project, a PERFORMANCE bond is expensive but is the best means to guarantee the insurance company's promise to the insured.

Sample Scope of Loss

This is an example of a professional Scope of Loss which details one room of a 1950s house lost in the 2003 California wildfires. In this case, the contractor used an industry standard estimating program called Xactimate. Figure 4 includes detail from one of the rooms in the house and Figure 5 is a category-by-category recap of that same house. Notice the bottom line of this scope is over $200,000. This homeowner was insured for just over $100,000.

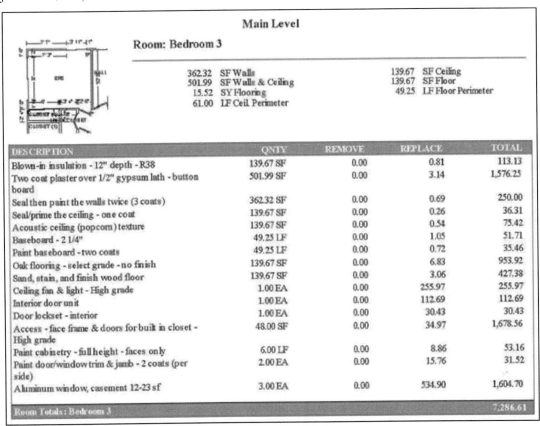

Figure 4: Sample Page of a Scope of Loss

Recap By Category		
O&P Items	**Total Dollars**	**%**
APPLIANCES	2,800.00	1.40%
AWNINGS & PATIO COVERS	213.40	0.11%
CABINETRY	4,293.55	2.14%
CLEANING	4,456.21	2.22%
CONCRETE	9,013.95	4.49%
GENERAL DEMOLITION	1,851.38	0.92%
DOORS	2,684.78	1.34%
DRYWALL	1,352.75	0.67%
ELECTRICAL	3,960.98	1.97%
EXCAVATION	3,457.05	1.72%
FLOOR COVERING - CERAMIC TILE	787.53	0.39%
FLOOR COVERING - VINYL	640.71	0.32%
FLOOR COVERING - WOOD	7,967.35	3.97%
FINISH CARPENTRY / TRIMWORK	5,295.54	2.64%
FINISH HARDWARE	556.85	0.28%
FRAMING & ROUGH CARPENTRY	23,328.64	11.63%
HEAT, VENT & AIR CONDITIONING	2,690.95	1.34%
INSULATION	831.41	0.41%
LABOR ONLY	25,879.20	12.90%
LIGHT FIXTURES	1,279.85	0.64%
MASONRY	1,294.00	0.65%
INTERIOR LATH & PLASTER	12,539.16	6.25%
PLUMBING	5,576.34	2.78%
PAINTING	4,750.98	2.37%
ROOFING	2,770.47	1.38%
SIDING	238.08	0.12%
SPECIALTY ITEMS	5,036.52	2.51%
STUCCO & EXTERIOR PLASTER	5,270.12	2.63%
TILE	847.23	0.42%
TEMPORARY REPAIRS	2,679.25	1.34%
WINDOWS - ALUMINUM	5,903.32	2.94%
WALLPAPER	37.10	0.02%
Subtotal	150,284.65	74.92%
O&P Items Subtotal	185,106.64	92.28%
Non-O&P Items	**Total Dollars**	**%**
GENERAL DEMOLITION	6,720.00	3.35%
PERMITS AND FEES	8,775.00	4.37%
Non-O&P Items Subtotal	15,495.00	7.72%
O&P Items Subtotal	185,106.64	92.28%
Grand Total	200,601.64	

Figure 5: A Sample Recap from a Scope of Loss

Like Kind and Quality

Knowing or finding the details of the construction of your home can make a huge difference in the settlement process. The price difference between plaster walls and a raised foundation, compared to drywall and concrete, can be tens of thousands of dollars for your bottom line.

Like kind and quality is a description of a replacement product or building material equal to what you had. Not all paint, tile or wallpaper is the same kind, quality or cost. Items priced by an insurer's computer program tend to be generic, low-cost products that, if a homeowner doesn't know the difference, might be substituted for the higher quality or custom items that were actually in the lost house. This is especially important when you have custom materials such as solid hardwood floors, plaster walls and ceilings, or locally quarried stone.

Some policies use this term right in their policy, while other homeowners must rely on the insurance code when referring to this term during the settlement process. Here is an example of the term used in a policy:

In consideration of the premium charged, Item **b.** of the **Loss Settlement** provision of the **Section I - Conditions** is entirely deleted and replaced by:

b. Buildings under Coverage A or B will have covered property losses settled, subject to the following:
  (1) We will pay the cost to repair or replace the building with material of like kind and quality, after application of the deductible and without deduction for depreciation, not to exceed the least of the following amounts:

    (a) The full replacement cost of the dwelling or other structures for like construction and use up to 150% of the limit shown on the Declarations Page; or
    (b) The necessary amount actually spent to repair the damaged building.

Figure 6: 2007 Renewal of a Wawanesa Policy

The California Department of Insurance defines Replacement Cost Coverage as follows:

> **Replacement Cost Coverage:** provides a dollar amount to repair damaged property or to replace it with new property of *like kind and quality*, without deducting for depreciation (that is, the decrease in value due to age, obsolescence, wear and tear and other factors.)[18]

This means if the dwelling had plaster walls, single-paned aluminum windows and hardwood floors, you need to value those items without regard for what you plan to do with your new house.

Having an understanding of these terms is important because you should be reimbursed for the value of what you had and for what you were originally insured.

---

[18] 11/8/10. *http://www.insurance.ca.gov/0100-consumers/0060-information-guides/0040-residential/tip-homeowner-insur.cfm#replacement.* Emphasis added.

Line of Sight Rule

When repairing property that is partially damaged, you might find that you and your adjuster disagree on *what type* and/or *how much* replacement or repair of materials is required. In general, do not accept repairs that fail to restore the damaged item to its pre-loss condition, or which leave it non-uniform in appearance. Unfortunately, there is no hard and fast rule that strictly defines "what type" or "how much," but an understanding of the standards can help you get your property back to its previous condition.

> "...do not accept repairs that fail to restore the damaged item to its pre-loss condition, or which leave it non-uniform in appearance."

Uniform and **Clear Line of Sight** define the extent of repair. California Insurance Code §2695.9(a)(2) should be referred to when looking for guidance, as it states:

"When a loss requires replacement of items and the replaced items do not match in quality, color or size, the insurer shall replace all items in the damaged area so as to conform to a reasonably uniform appearance."

Uniform means repair work should not be unreasonably noticeable after completion. The results should be identical (and can even be better) than before the damage. For example, they can't replace a few broken pink tiles with white tiles. Even if they were to find pink tile, it's not uncommon for all of the tile to be replaced due to the natural variations in tile, the way in which colors and surfaces change over time, and the difficulty in matching new grouting to old. Having even slightly different colored tiles would make the area no longer "conform to a reasonably uniform appearance."

Since "reasonable" is a subjective term, you will find yourself negotiating again with the adjuster. The adjuster's idea of "reasonable" will be guided by company requirements. Your "reasonable" will be informed by the fact that you knew what your house looked like before the damage.

Clear Line of Sight, while not explicitly cited, can be inferred from "the insurer shall replace all items in the damaged area." It is generally recognized that this means the insurance company will pay to replace all materials or surfaces that you can clearly see in your line of sight, i.e. that are in the same room and/or are contiguous. For example, if you have the same wall-to-wall carpet in your house and part of the carpet is damaged, they should replace all carpet that is not only in the same room, but all the way to a natural break where you no longer see the same carpet. Closing a door may not be a natural break as the door is generally open most of the time. Negotiating a "natural break" could prove to be a hot topic between you and your adjuster.

These two standards are closely related, but breaking them down might help you clarify the issues.

For example: Your house suffers water damage from a broken pipe requiring all of the drywall in your house to be removed two feet from floor. You want to make sure that once the damage has been fixed, the repair is not obvious. Should an adjuster convince you that furniture will cover any remaining distortions or non-uniform areas, the standard has not been met because you may decide later that you want to rearrange your furniture, which will reveal the substandard repair.

Also, if you had special drywall or an uncommon texture that is difficult to duplicate, additional measures would need to be implemented so the result is "reasonably uniform in appearance" throughout the room. The contractor would need to re-texture and re-paint all of the walls in the damaged room to completely remove the water line.

One last point: be certain that the reasonable uniform surface repair will be PERMANENT or at least continue to look similar to the adjoining unrepaired surfaces. Just because it looks good today does not mean it will be the same a year from now. If different materials are used, exposure to sun, rain, and general wear and tear can cause different materials to age quite differently.

For example, paint stores have computers which can match paint colors. However, if paint repairs are made just to a small patched area, over time the differences between the non-damages surface and the newly painted patch tends to stick out like a sore thumb. Our advice to avoid this is to negotiate repainting of the entire wall and/or room.

Another example is broken tile. Some homeowners maintain extra tiles in case of loss and offer the tile to maintain a reasonably uniform surface. Be careful. Sometimes the grout between tiles cannot be duplicated and the tile repair sticks out like a sore thumb. Beware too: a small tile repair can compromise the water barrier behind or beneath the tile. (This example invokes the "pre-loss condition" rule.)

Repairs typically associated with the clear line of sight rule are:

- Carpet (or other floor coverings)
- Paint (or other floor covering)
- Tile
- Doors (especially when the doors match throughout the house)
- Windows (remember they need to match inside and out)
- Trim and molding
- Roofing
- Fencing

What is Depreciable in the Dwelling Coverage?

Depreciation was defined in detail on page 46, but understanding **what is actually depreciable** is an important part of the settlement process.

In general, items that show regular wear and tear, or that are replaceable, are depreciable. California Insurance Code §2051 states

> *"...a deduction for physical depreciation shall apply only to components of a structure that are normally subject to repair and replacement during the useful life of that structure."*

This includes items such as flooring, roofing and wall coverings including paint and wallpaper. Items that are not depreciable include things like the studs and the foundation, for example.

Another item that cannot be depreciated is labor. The California Fair Settlement Practice Regulations of 2006 states:

> *California Insurance Code §2659.9 (f)(1) "...Except for the intrinsic labor costs that are included in the cost of manufactured materials or goods, the expense of labor necessary to repair, rebuild or replace covered property is not a component of physical depreciation and shall not be subject to depreciation or betterment."*

This can be a bit trickier to find as labor is sometimes bundled in with the repair. For example, here is a copy of an actual quote for a roof repair:

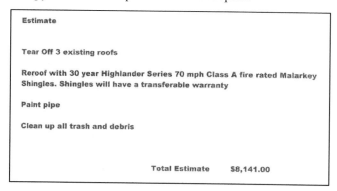

Figure 7: Roof Repair Estimate

Let's say the roof had a life span of 20 years and was 10 years old at the time of the repair. The insurance company proposes to give you $4,070 as the depreciated value (half of the bid since the life of the roof is half over). It might sound reasonable at first, until you ask the contractor to break down the costs of the estimate.

Labor:	$4,000	$4,000 (not depreciable)
Material:	$2,000	$1,000 (depreciated by half)
Haul Away:	$1,000	$1,000 (not depreciable)
Soft Costs & profit:	$1,141	$1,141 (not depreciable)
Total:	**$8,141**	**$7,141 total up-front payment owed**

In this case only the costs of the materials (or $2,000) can be depreciated and the initial payment to the homeowner should be $7,141 and not $4,070.

Another technique some adjusters use is to blame the covered loss for the depreciation. Do not let them convince you that the item is unusable due to the loss and therefore has no value or has significantly more depreciation. You are always to be paid based on the item's value prior to the loss.

In the end, remember that regardless of how straight forward and mathematical depreciation might seem – *depreciation is always negotiable*.

And if you have a replacement policy, don't forget to collect the depreciated amount (the $1,000 held back in this example) from the insurance company once the repair is complete.

> *"...don't forget to collect the depreciated amount from the insurance company once the repair is complete."*

Sketching Your Own As-Built Floor Plan

A **floor plan** is one of the first things you'll need to determine the cost of reconstructing your home. It's great if you were able to find one from another source, but most people aren't that lucky. If you need to create your own floor plan, here are some tips.

Materials you'll need:

- Graph paper (or, if you're adventurous, you can use an inexpensive computer program).
- Clipboard
- Pencil and eraser
- Long tape measure
- Camera
- Container(s) to hold remnants of your house (trash bags, large plastic storage boxes, etc.)
- Protective gear for working around the site (mask, gloves, goggles, heavy shoes, etc.)

Now you can start sketching. Here is an example, to help you with some of the symbols commonly used when creating a floor plan:

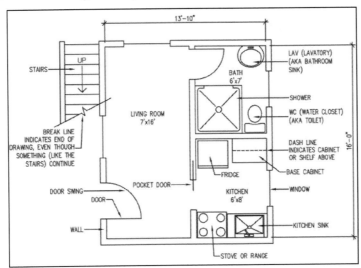

Figure 8: Sample Floor Plan with Symbology Called Out

1. Find the overall dimensions of your house by measuring the foundation. Calculate each square on your graph paper as one foot. Draw the outline of your house based on your measurements and write each measurement next to the line you draw. Please

note that your house might extend an inch or so on each side of your foundation. Check undamaged homes around your neighborhood for reference.

2. Walk through your house, measuring what you can to recreate the size of each room (use nails or other fasteners embedded in the concrete that held down the walls, plumbing fixtures or remaining appliances, etc.) If nothing else, pace out what you can and measure it, drawing walls as you go. Remembering the size of furniture that fit in the room might help.

3. Take pictures of any part of what's left of your house that helps prove your loss.

4. Pull actual samples out of the rubble, and be prepared to save it until you have completely settled your claim (i.e. you have signed a settlement agreement or moved into your new house). You'll especially want to take anything that represents unusual or custom construction. Examples might be a part of the plaster walls, tile samples, electrical conduit or a special sink fixture. (Please see "Before You Remove the Debris" on page 17 for more information on why you'll need this.)

5. Take pictures of anything you don't take with you. For example, the raised foundation footings.

6. Collect pictures of your house, inside and out. Ask friends and relatives for pictures if you lost all of yours in the disaster. You might find that your memory is jogged by seeing details in the background. (As in: "Oh yeah, there was a closet right there!")

7. If there are any other houses in your area that are the same as yours, use that house as a reference.

8. Find a satellite image of your house. This can help to place the house on the property, define the roof and/or compare the size of the house you draw to the actual house in the photo.

Draw as much as possible, but don't stress yourself out about being perfect with your "art work." The professional you use to complete your Scope of Loss will probably use it as a reference to do a much more thorough job, but since they were unable to see the house prior to the loss, any information you can provide will be invaluable.

Chapter 6 **Personal Property Coverage**

Retail outlets to aid in listing and valuing your personal inventory losses

☐ Grocery Store: _____

☐ Drug Store: _____

☐ Big Box Store: _____

☐ Department Store: _____

☐ Garden Store: _____

☐ Hardware Store: _____

☐ Clothing Store: _____

☐ Toy Store: _____

☐ Kid's Store: _____

☐ Furniture Store: _____

☐ Antique Store: _____

☐ Electronics Store: _____

☐ Craft Store: _____

☐ Kitchen Store: _____

☐ Beauty Supply: _____

☐ Candle Store: _____

☐ Adult Items: _____

☐ Sports Memorabilia: _____

☐ Shoe Store: _____

☐ Leather goods: _____

☐ _____ : _____

☐ _____ :: _____

☐ _____ :: _____

☐ _____ :: _____

☐ _____ :: _____

☐ _____ :: _____

☐ _____ :: _____

☐ _____ :: _____

☐ _____ :: _____

☐ _____ :: _____

☐ _____ :: _____

☐ _____ :: _____

Tasks for This Chapter

☐ Obtain a copy of the personal property inventory guide provided by CARe. You can download it from our website at www.carehelp.org.

☐ You can print out the guide or use the interactive spreadsheet and update it as often as necessary.

☐ Go through the spreadsheet and delete the items you know for a fact you did not have.

☐ Throughout the process you will probably think of things to add to your list. Get a small notebook or another method to log these items as you think of them.

☐ Make a goal to sit down for at least a short period of time every day to add things to, or do additional research for, your list.

☐ To help jog your memory, refer to the section "Creating Your Personal Property Inventory" on page 69.

☐ Start turning in parts of your inventory to your insurance company. See page 74 for help with preparing partial lists of your inventory.

Creating Your Personal Property Inventory

If your insurance company requires an inventory (though with large disasters some do not require it), doing your **personal property inventory** list after a total (or near total) loss, can be one of the most difficult tasks after a disaster.

It also encompasses a large portion of your monetary claim. And although some policies can range from a dollar amount on some specialty policies, or percentages ranging from 25 percent to 100 percent of Dwelling Coverage (or Coverage A), most California policies include personal property coverage which equals between 70 percent and 75 percent of Coverage A. This means that for the majority of policyholders, for every $100,000 in dwelling coverage, you have an additional $70,000 to $75,000 in personal property coverage. Your declarations page should show your limit.

The problem is, simply thinking about listing from memory each and every item you owned can seem absolutely overwhelming. Take heart, you're not alone. We hope to make this task a bit easier to tackle and complete in a timely manner. Here are a few tips:

- **Start now**: The longer you wait, the more you will forget and the harder it will be to start.

> *Start now: The longer you wait, the more you will forget and the harder it will be to start.*

- Do not wait until you are "done" with your list to start claiming personal property items and collecting your money. **Turn in pages of your inventory on a regular basis and start collecting money now**. You should know that this task will probably never be "done." Years from now you will think of something you forgot to put on your list, but by doing as much as possible now you can minimize this.

- Ask (in writing) for a waiver on your policy's 180-day replacement provision (for a sample letter see page 34).

- If your adjuster gives you an inventory form with several columns of information to fill out about each item, review your policy to determine which columns are required and which aren't. (See "Sample Inventory Form from an Insurance Company," page 71.)

- Use our Sample Inventory with thousands of examples of things that might have been in your home. Download from our website at www.carehelp.org. (See also "Starting Your Inventory" on page 72.)

- List everything. Yes, we mean everything. You will end up with thousands of dollars of items that each cost less than $5. Consider this story by Frank Dumas which is included in his book *Claim Paid*:

> *A friend of mine had a toolbox stolen from his car. He asked me to look over his loss report before sending it in to the insurance company. He had written down 'One toolbox containing miscellaneous hand tools' and placed a value of $250 on his loss. I asked him to prepare a full description of the toolbox, including the size and number of trays. Then I told him to get a lined note pad and go through a Sears catalogue, or similar book listing tools, writing down each separate item that was in the tool box to the best of his recollection and pricing each article individually.*
>
> *The final list took up four single-spaced pages. The total value of the tool box and its contents when itemized came to almost $750. The claim was submitted to the insurer, which paid the claim in full without question. While the insured had been willing to settle his claim for $250, he received three times what he originally thought to be the value of his claim simply*

by following a procedure the insurance company understood and accepted.[19]

- Never use the original cost of the item. Always use today's replacement cost.

- For antiques or collectibles, ask an expert to give you a written estimate. Find a reputable dealer who is knowledgeable and can appraise the items from either photographs or your description. Don't be surprised if the dealer charges for his services, but make sure the charge is reasonable. Keep the receipt for the service charge and claim it as part of your ALE coverage.

- Potted plants (and the pots and dirt) can be claimed as personal property, especially if you would have taken them with you if you moved.

- If the insurance company only gives you the ACV up front, don't forget to collect the RCV once you've replaced the items. Many policies have replacement provisions that require you to prove you've replaced the item before you get the full reimbursement. *Keep the receipts* and create a schedule to turn them in to collect the difference.

- In some cases, if your home and contents were destroyed in a covered incident (i.e. fire), **all** of your personal property is covered, even antiques and collectibles. With some policies these items are not covered for theft without an added endorsement or rider, but are covered in case of fire.

- Include any taxes, shipping, handling delivery, installation, storage, setup and even delivery from your storage location to your completed house.

- Depreciation is ALWAYS negotiable.

- Carpets, drapery and light fixtures are subject to negotiation as to real or personal property.

To Help Remember the Things You Lost:

- Try drawing a diagram of each room. This does not have to be an accurate drawing and it's not something you even have to share with anyone. It is simply a mental exercise to help you remember what was in each room.

    1. Start with one room of your house.

    2. Divide a piece of paper into four squares (or one for each wall).

    3. Draw in approximately where doors and windows were positioned.

    4. Start drawing what was on each wall. For example, there might have been a chair with a side table near the wall. On the table there might have been a lamp (and the harp, shade and finial). The lamp had a light bulb and an extension cord. The extension cord was plugged into a three-way splitter at the outlet. The chair had a throw blanket, a pillow and a pouch where the remote control was stored. The remote control had two AA batteries. Continue on in this way.

- Try different games to think of things like "everything that starts with the letter 'P'," or "everything that is yellow," or "everything that is related to shoes."

- Ask anyone you know if they have pictures that were taken around your house (maybe from Thanksgiving or the last big bash you hosted).

> **TIP**: *use different mental exercises to help you remember what was in each room.*

---

[19] Dumas, Frank. *Claim Paid*. Stratton Press, 1989.

- Use catalogues, the internet, and gift registries to your advantage.

- Ask your local grocery store for a copy of their inventory. Use it to jog your memory (and share it with other disaster survivors in your area).

- Call stores and financial institutions which you had a previous relationship with *immediately* to request purchase histories or copies of statements. Do this as soon as possible. The longer you wait the more of the pre-disaster purchasing history is lost.

  o Call companies for which you have a frequent buyer card. Many companies keep detailed information on file for much longer than you would expect.

  o If you are a member at a warehouse store, ask them for a copy of your purchase history.

  o Call any company you have made a major purchase with and ask for receipts (and today's full retail price).

  o If you purchased items online, many times that information will be stored in your account for quite a while as well.

  o Call your credit card company and/or bank and ask for back statements. Request a waiver for any fees due to the circumstances. If they will not budge, make sure to keep a record of the costs and claim it as part of your ALE coverage.

  o For major purchases charged to a credit card, the issuing bank can request a copy of the receipt from the company you purchased the item from.

Sample Inventory Form from an Insurance Company

The following is an example of a form one might receive from an insurance company after a loss. Although we've seen many such examples, this one was found by searching the internet for "Personal Property Inventory Form."[20]

PERSONAL PROPERTY INVENTORY FORM

Room: _____ Page _____ of _____

Policy Number: _____ Claim Number: _____
Insured: _____ Date of Loss: _____

Qty	Description of Property (Include manufacturer, brand name, serial and model numbers)	Purchased or Obtained From	Date of Purchase or Age	Original Cost New	Method of Payment (Cash, Charge, etc.)	Current Replacement Cost	Cost of Repair or Restore	COMPANY USE ONLY Dept/Settlement Amount

Figure 9: Sample Insurance Industry Inventory Form

When you first sit down to fill out this form, the magnitude of your situation might start to kick in. You have to do this for every single solitary item in your house – every pencil and piano; every toothpick and tiara. This is going to take a lot of paper and a lot of research. But it might not be quite as bad as you think.

---

[20] 8/20/10. http://www.weabenefits.com/home/uploadedFiles/z_docs/Insurance/Forms/2561-Personal_Property_Inventory_Form.pdf

Although some policies require more than others, it's a safe bet that you won't need every piece of information included on the list above. Before you get started you need to pull out that copy of your policy. Look for a section called "Your Duties After Loss" which details what you need to do after a loss when you file a claim. The following are examples from two different insurance policies. The policy on the left requires more information be provided by the homeowner than the policy on the right.

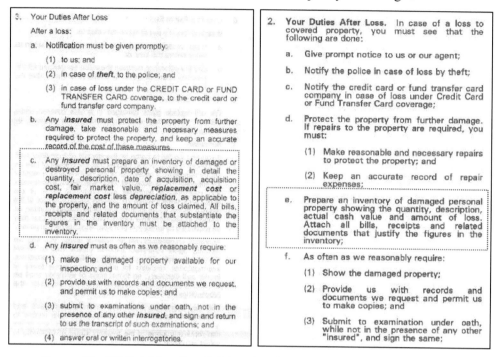

Figure 10: 2010 AAA policy (left) and a 2008 American Modern Policy (right)

Starting Your Inventory

Even if you have a policy that requires more than most, don't despair. In a total loss situation it might be impossible to provide information for every item, so just start with the basics. You can even use the Sample Inventory Excel Spreadsheet, located on the CARe website, which is already populated with thousands of items you might have had in your house. Here's what it looks like (prices not included in actual spreadsheet and are only shown for example purposes):

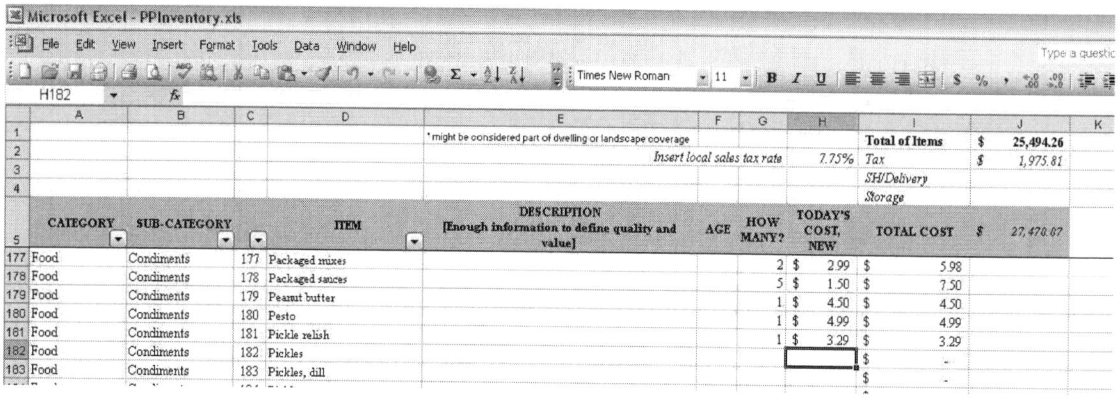

Figure 11: CARe, Inc. Sample Inventory Spreadsheet

You can start by simply going through the list and removing everything you are positive was *not* in your house. Once you've done that you will already have a pretty good start on your inventory.

The next step is to take your list and start including current prices.

Pricing Your Inventory

There is no central database available to a homeowner to price your inventory. You'll need to go and research prices at your local stores, or use the prices they have listed on their websites.

So, what is the best way to estimate prices, since they are constantly changing? Many people find that using wish lists or registries with stores or websites is a great way to quickly gather the needed information. Make sure you print the list when complete. If you go to a store to do this, they will likely hand you a scanner and let you walk around the store scanning everything you remember having and then let you print out the list before you leave the store. The benefit of using a registry is that the current pricing is listed next to each item. Keep this documentation until your claim is closed.

You should also start with the tips on page 45 as soon as possible.

For hard to price items (one-of-a-kind or antiques) find a specialty store or website that can help. It might be difficult to find, but there is always someone out there who can help price your item (think Antiques Roadshow or Pawn Stars).

As a warning, in some situations your adjuster might ask for proof of your pricing (and sometimes not until *way* down the line). You might notice that the sample policies above request that all documentation be attached to justify your inventory. While most people immediately think this documentation refers to a justification of what they had prior to the fire (and this does happen as well), some adjusters take this to mean justifying your pricing. Although you may not need to include any attached proof in your initial submittal, if you do not save or print the pricing you get from stores or the internet you can find yourself in a real bind down the road, if they ask for it. We've seen them ask for documentation for both low- and high-priced items. The more documentation you have, the stronger your claim and the safer you'll feel knowing you have a strong claim that can withstand scrutiny by the insurance company.

Describing Your Inventory

Don't spend an excessive amount of time describing your inventory. A brief description of each item should suffice. If they want more information, they will let you know.

Turning in Your Inventory to the Insurance Company

Numbering the Pages for Less Confusion

Once you've completed a few pages of your inventory you can turn it in so you can start collecting from your claim. It is a good idea to number every item and every page of your inventory. Also, add the date to each page. This way every item is easily referenced later on (for example, if you look at item number 4 on page 5 of the inventory dated July 15, 2009...)

Once You Turn in Your Inventory

Continue your research on items you remembered since you turned in your last list.

Once you turn your inventory in to the insurance company, they will "process" it. Usually this means it is sent to an inventory specialty company that will input the data using their own generic descriptions and pricing. In most cases, a printout of this revised inventory is returned back to you.

Sometimes you won't get the inventory back immediately but you will start to get questions about the pages you turned in. They might want more detail about an item or proof of your pricing. If you've remembered to keep these items as you collected the information it should be a fairly straightforward (though time consuming) matter to get it back to them.

If You Find Mistakes

When you get your inventory back, your next step is to compare the inventory you completed to the one that was returned to you. Any mistakes you find should be reported back to the insurance company. Mistakes might include missing items, excessive depreciation, changed replacement cost, etc.

Things That Have Internal Limits and Coverage "Riders"

Some items might be removed from the inventory. If the reason given is they are not covered without a rider, the individual who sent the letter might have mistaken a theft claim for a disaster claim. Research this topic; in some cases, if your home and contents were destroyed in a covered peril (i.e. fire), all of your personal property is covered, even antiques and collectibles. Theft is a different matter.

Depreciation on Personal Property Items

TIP: Depreciation is negotiable.

In almost all cases where the insurance company requires an inventory, issues will arise around the depreciation they come up with. Usually they have some generic database that is used for every claimant in the United States with slight variations for pricing due to zip code. This is why you should check the depreciation and contest it if you deem it necessary.

You should know that some items, including antiques, art work, collectibles and other specialty items do **NOT** depreciate. In these instances, RCV and ACV may be equal, and often increase in value since acquisition. You may need your own qualified professional – not your claims adjuster or the adjuster's computer – to establish your true values.

Please be aware that the insurance company is required to document their depreciation of your items. From the Fair Claim Settlement Practice Regulation:

California Insurance Code §2695.9 (f) When the amount claimed is adjusted because of betterment, depreciation, or salvage, all justification for the adjustment shall be contained in the claim file. Any adjustments shall be discernable, measurable, itemized, and specified as to dollar amount, and shall accurately reflect the value of the betterment, depreciation, or salvage. Any adjustment for betterment or depreciation shall reflect a measurable difference in market value attributable to the condition and age of the property and apply only to property normally subject to repair and replacement during the useful life of the property. The basis for any adjustment shall be fully explained to the claimant in writing.

Don't Forget Your Hold Back

Do not forget additional settlement money that may remain within the policy coverages that you did not initially receive – unpaid depreciated funds or **hold back**. RJ Atherton explains the process in his book *The Claim Game*:

> *"The standard procedure is to pay you the ACV of the loss as the first stop. Then once you show that you have rebuilt [or replaced] the property, the insurance company will pay you the balance of the difference between actual cash value and replacement cost value. If you elect not to rebuild [or replace], you'll just receive the ACV."*[21]

For example, a homeowner with $150,000 in personal property coverage may have submitted an inventory of $200,000. The insurance company depreciated the value of all reported items and only paid $130,000. The homeowner has $20,000 of personal property coverage remaining within the policy limits.

What can be done to claim the additional unpaid settlement funds?

1. Continue writing and submitting the personal property list.

Include all the little, inexpensive items. It all adds up and small necessities often are the first things replaced (and first things forgotten), so the adjuster should give its full value up front. Think of that first trip to the mega-mart, taken right after the fire. Buying all new toothbrushes, toothpaste, shampoo, deodorants, razors, and other toiletries creates a large bill all by themselves.

Spend some time and itemize areas that were grouped together or categorized. For example, if you claimed a group of items using a lump sum price -– like a tool box, a sewing box, or gardening items – break the category down and itemize to determine their full value, including the cost of the containers or boxes. Based on our experience with disasters, you will be amazed at the full cost!

2. Claim withheld depreciation.

For instance, you claimed a $2,000 couch and the insurance company paid only $1,000 as the depreciated amount. You then bought a "like-kind-and- quality" couch at a cost of $2,100 (don't forget tax and delivery). Send the receipt to the insurance company and claim payment for the "hold back"– an additional $1100. You can do this on an item-by-item basis.

3. Negotiate any item that was excessively depreciated.

In the above example, the couch was depreciated 50 percent – an unusually high depreciation. Depreciation, based on the wear and tear or physical condition, is always negotiable. Only you know the actual condition at the time of loss. Negotiate a

> *"Include all the little, inexpensive items. It all adds up and small necessities often are the first things replaced (and first things forgotten)"*

---

[21] Atherton, RJ. *The Claim Game.* Lambert & Morris Pr, 1992.

reduced depreciated amount if the item has been excessively depreciated. For example, if you just purchased the couch or the item was rarely used and was in excellent condition, or was an antique or a collectible. We have seen many items overly depreciated by the arbitrary judgment of the adjuster or the technical application of a computer. Remember, only you know the condition of an item, not an "in-house" chart or a computer.

Special Considerations for Partial Losses

- Carefully do your OWN documentation of items before the pack out (when a restoration company packs your items and sends them out to be cleaned or repaired).

- Make sure a local company is used so you can easily access your items.

- Make sure that your items are nearby so you have easy and quick access to them. We have seen pack outs put in storage two or more hours away – in good traffic. You need them close to you!

- Make sure you're charged a *reasonable* amount for storage after the items have been cleaned, but before your house is ready.

See also the section in Chapter 5 titled "Consider looking over the list of earthquake damages since strong winds might produce some of the same results.

- Problems Associated with Cleaning Smoke" on page 24.

Chapter 7 **Living Expense, Debris Removal & Other Coverages**

Other coverages to collect on

☐ ALE

☐ Debris removal

Debris removal contractors to interview: _____

_____

_____

_____

☐ Other structures

Other structures on my property include: _____

_____

_____

_____

☐ Building code upgrade

☐ Landscape (trees, shrubs, plants and lawns)

☐ Fire Department service charge

☐ Identity fraud

☐ Power interruption/food spoilage

☐ Lock re-keying

☐ Temporary repairs after a loss

☐ Land stabilization

☐ Damage created during repairs

☐ Other: _____

☐ Other: _____

☐ Other: _____

☐ Other: _____

☐ Other: _____

Tasks For This Chapter

☐ Become familiar with expenses associated with ALE (Additional Living Expenses or Loss of Use) coverage. See page 79.

☐ Make a knowledgeable decision on where you want to live based on your limits and budget. See "Appropriate Temporary Living Arrangements" on page 80.

☐ Understand how much Debris Removal coverage you have. See page 82.

☐ Make a list of those things that might be considered part of "Other Structures Coverage." See page 83.

☐ Look at your policy to determine if you have Building Code Upgrade coverage. See page 84.

☐ Look at your policy to determine if there are any other coverages that apply to your loss. See page 86.

Additional Living Expenses

Additional Living Expenses, sometimes shortened to **ALE** or called **Loss of Use**, is coverage for any expenses incurred following a covered loss which are above and beyond your normal living expenses.

For example, your house is damaged by a fire and is considered uninhabitable. You go to a hotel for a few nights while researching a replacement house. During this time you must eat out all three meals every day. 100 percent of the hotel bill should be covered. The insurance company may argue that they only have to pay for a certain percentage of your meals (since eating out generally costs more than at home), but some will initially pay 100 percent of your meals while you're eating out as well.

> *TIP: Additional living expenses can also be called ALE or Loss of Use.*

Limits to your Living Expense Coverage

Some policies are limited by a dollar amount, some are limited by time and some are limited by both. In California the time limit is extended for survivors of a declared natural disaster from the standard 12 months to 24 months.

> *California Insurance Code §2060 states: "If a state of emergency has been declared, coverage for additional living expenses shall be for a period of 24 months. Insurers[sic] must provide homeowner/insureds with a list of items that are covered by the 'additional living expense' part of the insurance policy."[22]*

If your policy has a dollar amount limit, this 12-month extension does not increase the amount of coverage available to you, only the length of time in which you have to spend it.

Read your dec page and policy carefully to determine what limits exist for you. Please know your limits and plan for them far in advance.

Examples of Items Covered by ALE

- Hotel expenses: tips, dining out, parking.

- "Moral" obligation to pay for housing with friends or relatives (according to AICPCU). Have your friend or relative write a rental receipt and allow them to be compensated for the inconvenience.

- Additional driving mileage (see current IRS or AAA mileage rates).

- Childcare expenses *above normal expenses.*

- House cleaning service *above normal expenses.*

- Cost to install and hookup fees for cable and utilities.

- Cost to install phone and forward number to temporary addresses.

- Cell phone, telephone, postage costs above normal expenses.

- Utility bills to temporary power poles might be charged at a higher rate than normal residential rates. The *difference* between your old bill and the new bill.

---

[22] 04/05/11. http://www.insurance.ca.gov/wf-con-info/0020-ho-rights/

- Extra supplies related to living in an RV such as toilet chemicals and difference between the price of regular toilet paper and the special toilet paper you might need to use in an RV.

- Long distance phone calls to insurance company.

- Pet boarding.

- Meals while in hotel or moving *above normal expenses.*

- Laundry and dry cleaning *above normal expenses.*

- Costs related to documentation of dwelling, personal property losses.

- Files, paper, notebook and diary costs related to insurance claim. (These are not personal property replacements but directly related to additional expenses due to the loss.)

- Expenses related to replacement of licenses, diplomas, certificates, passports.

- Storage of replacement contents.

If you choose to live in a trailer on your lot during construction

There are often regulations regarding living on your property in a trailer following a disaster. Please contact the municipality in which you reside regarding the steps they require for this option. Here are some expenses that should be covered by ALE:

- Some insurance companies will pay for purchasing a trailer while others balk at purchasing an asset with money that is supposed to be for expenses only. *NOTE: purchasing an asset with ALE money might have tax ramifications. Please discuss this with your accountant or CPA prior to completing the transaction.* Some survivors rent trailers from friends or relatives. If you do this, check around for the current rental rate of a trailer and have your friend or relative write a rental agreement for the going rate.

- Installation fees of a temporary electric pole (the cable company might also use this pole).

- Cost per KWh delivered to a pole is often more expensive than to a house. The utility might charge business rates to a temporary pole. Some survivors after a disaster have been successful in convincing the electric company to reduce the rate to a temporary pole, so don't hesitate to ask. Compare your before and after bills to see if your overall bill is higher than before.

- Supplies used in a trailer that are not usually required such as toilet chemicals and special toilet paper.

- Services to a trailer such as gas delivery or sewage dumping.

Appropriate Temporary Living Arrangements

Before you start looking for temporary (which many times turns into long term) quarters, you should determine the limits of your ALE coverage. See "Limits to your Living Expense Coverage" on page 79.

While looking for a temporary replacement home, remember, you are entitled to "like kind and quality" or to continue your "normal standard of living." In your policy the language might read something like:

> **We** will pay the reasonable increase in living expenses necessary to maintain **your** <u>normal standard of living</u> when a direct physical loss **we** cover makes **your** **residence premises** uninhabitable.

Figure 12: ALE in an Allstate Deluxe HO Policy

If you had a 1,700-square-foot home with four bedrooms and three baths with a pool, a two-bedroom condo is not equivalent, even if it is 1,700 square feet with a common pool. Living in a condo with a public pool is not the same as living in a single family dwelling with a private pool. If you decide a condo is okay, then that is your choice, but don't feel forced into that situation.

Remember, it may be only temporary but it may be two or more years before your return to your new home. Two years is a LONG time. Ask yourself: "Will I (we) be comfortable living here for the next two years?"

Look for a house with *your* amenities such as:

- Pool
- Landscaping
- Workshop
- Sewing room
- Exercise room
- Gourmet kitchen

> *"...get as short a lease as possible... even if you've come to the conclusion that it will take two years to replace your house."*

Furnish your house with "like kind and quality" furnishings such as:

- Art work
- Antiques
- Piano
- Pool table

It is always a good idea to get as short a lease as possible in this situation, even if you've come to the conclusion that it will take two years to replace your house. You don't want to find yourself locked into a living situation that proves too expensive, or inappropriate in some other way.

Keep ALE Receipts Separate

Each portion of your claim has a separate limit, and receipts for each of these sections should be kept separately. ALE is settled on an "as incurred" basis meaning that you have to pay for the expense up-front before you are reimbursed.

After a disaster you are often given an advance to spend as needed. Even though it is often spent on Additional Living Expenses, these advances are often advances on Personal Property coverage. Ultimately you must always document how you spent your advance, including ALE expenses or risk losing a portion of your claim.

Different Ways to Calculate ALE

There are two different ways to calculate ALE. One is by calculating Additional Living Expenses and the other is using the Fair Rental Value.

To calculate the Additional Living Expense, you first must determine what your regular living expenses are. Collect a history of your spending (utilities, fuel, transportation, etc.) and track your monthly budget. You then compare it to your new expenses. Anything above and beyond your normal spending would be considered Additional Living Expenses.

The second way is to find the Fair Rental Value of the damaged house. You will need to determine the rental value of your furnished house prior to the loss. Find a real estate broker who is familiar with rentals in your neighborhood to help determine this amount. Don't forget furniture.

Although most people assume ALE starts the day your house became uninhabitable, it has been argued the time – 12 months or 24 months – listed in your policy, should begin once the claim is fully settled. Unfortunately, you will have to do some serious negotiating to get the insurance company to agree with you on this.

NOTE: Unspent ALE funds may be treated as ordinary income by the IRS.

Debris Removal Coverage

Debris Removal Coverage includes the expenses associated with removing damaged, unsalvageable property from the lot. It is very important to document your loss prior to removing the evidence. *Before you move forward with removing the debris from the lot, please refer to Chapter 2 "Before You Remove the Debris."*

The limits of the debris removal coverage are generally calculated with a percentage of the limits of your "covered property." Most policies have 5 percent debris removal coverage, but check your policy to see what your percentage is.

> **2. Debris Removal.** We will pay the reasonable expense incurred by you in the removal of debris of covered property provided coverage is afforded for the peril causing the loss. This additional coverage does not include the cost of disposal, testing or storage of any hazardous or toxic materials. Debris removal expense is included in the limit of liability applying to the damaged property. When the amount payable for the actual damage to the property plus the expense for debris removal exceeds the limit of liability for the damaged property, an additional 5% of that limit of liability will be available to cover debris removal expense.

Figure 13: Debris Removal in a Century National Policy 2008 Renewal

Most policies pay 5 percent above the coverage amount of all "*covered property.*" This means that you should have available to you not only 5 percent of the dwelling coverage, but 5 percent of the other structures, personal property and landscaping coverages. This could make a huge difference in the funds available for debris removal. Here is an example:

Dwelling only		All covered property	
Dwelling Coverage	$200,000	Dwelling Coverage	$200,000
		Other Structures	20,000
		Personal Property	100,000
Coverage Sub-total	*$200,000*	*Coverage Sub-total*	*$320,000*
5% of sub-total	**$10,000**	**5% of sub-total**	**$16,000**

You might also note that debris removal coverage is not normally paid until the cost has been incurred, which means you have to pay up front and be reimbursed by the insurance company later.

Tree Removal

Landscape removal (which is usually covered under "Trees, Shrubs, Plants and Lawns") is usually listed as a separate coverage. See "Landscape Coverage (Trees, Shrubs, Plants and Lawns)" on page 85 for more information.

Other Structures Coverage

The limit of **Other Structures** (also called **Appurtenant Structures**) is generally a percentage (10 percent) of the Dwelling coverage. Unfortunately, for some people the cost to repair or replace damaged Other Structures can cost much more.

Deciding which portions of your dwelling are "Dwelling" and which are "Other Structures" can be very useful to homeowners running up against their limits in one category, but not the other. Read your policy very carefully under the "Dwelling" portion of the Coverages section. You will see a clause similar to this:

> **Your dwelling** including attached structures.
> Structures connected to **your dwelling** by only a fence, utility line, or similar connection are not considered attached structures.

Figure 14: Dwelling Definition in an Allstate Deluxe HO Policy

Attached/connected, means:

- In contact with
- Affixed
- Fastened
- Joined
- Stuck on
- Appended

> TIP: Other Structures coverage can also be called Appurtenant Structures.

Any structure, then, that is "in contact with"[23] your dwelling should be covered under your "Dwelling" and not "Other Structure." Examples of Dwelling Structures could include patios, decks, stairs and portions of supporting retaining walls.

Your "Other Structures" clause will read something like:

> Structures at the address shown on the Policy Declarations separated from **your dwelling** by clear space.
> Structures attached to **your dwelling** by only a fence, utility line, or similar connection.

Figure 15: Other Structures Definition in an Allstate Deluxe HO Policy

To be considered an Other Structure, the item has to be *separated* and connected by *only* a fence, utility line or similar connection.

Examples of Other Structures might include, a pool and the deck, a shed or completely detached (not connected as listed above) garage, fencing surrounding a pet enclosure or a gazebo.

---

[23] Department of Insurance Manual, 1989, Page 118

Building Code Upgrade Coverage

Building Code Upgrade coverage is an additional coverage purchased by the homeowner. If available, this coverage applies to the dwelling when the local municipality imposes new building standards which were not present in the existing dwelling.

> *"Depending on policy language, the Building Code Upgrade percentage should also apply to the replacement extension percentage of Coverage A."*

The limit of Building Code Upgrade coverage, also called **Ordinance or Law (or OL)**, is generally calculated with a percentage of Dwelling coverage. This coverage is usually additional coverage (ranging from 5 percent to as high as 100 percent of Coverage A).

Sometimes Building Code Upgrade coverage is *built into* the Dwelling coverage, which means it does not increase the dollar amount beyond your existing Dwelling coverage. It is important to read your policy to see which you have.

Depending on policy language, the Building Code Upgrade percentage should also apply to the replacement extension percentage of Coverage A. (Please see examples on page 41 for more information.)

A few policies also have Building Code Upgrade coverage on Other Structures, but most do not.

Building Code Upgrade coverage is one of the most confusing areas of insurance coverage for homeowners to understand – and to collect on. We have seen building code upgrade coverage applied differently depending on the policy language:

- To cover only code changes enacted *after* the original construction of your house, but *prior* to the <u>renewal date</u> OR <u>loss event</u> of your policy (which excludes *any* building code changes made after the date your policy was issued to you OR the house was lost).

- To cover any and all code changes enacted *after* the original construction of your house including any building code changes and enforcement after, and generally as a result of, your loss event.

The application most beneficial to your reconstruction depends on the amount of building code upgrades required by your municipality, the amount of Building Code Upgrade and/or Dwelling coverage you have, your ability to negotiate beyond policy limits and, of course, specific policy language.

Some insurers try to reduce your overall dwelling settlement by placing a portion of your rebuilding costs into your Ordinance or Law upgrades. This will make your Building Code Upgrade coverage seem insufficient.

Once you've determined how your insurance company interprets Building Code Upgrade coverage, you'll need to determine which items of the newly repaired or constructed home were "upgrades" to the dwelling due solely to a new building code. The cost of those items are tallied up and removed from the Dwelling coverage and reimbursed using Building Code Upgrade funds. In this way you will determine how much of the limit you are due.

You will most likely need to work with your contractor, engineer or architect to identify and price the appropriate Building Code Upgrades for your replacement dwelling. Examples of these items might include:

- Fire sprinklers (including upgrading water service to make them function)

- Additional structural items (rebar, hold-downs, etc.)

- Upgraded foundation

- Engineered walls (shear panels or Simpson Strong Walls)

- Upgraded doors or windows (including tempered glass)

- Changed roof venting requirements

- Change in lumber to accommodate new fire resistive laws

- Treated lumber in different areas of construction

- Enhanced treatment of the soil surrounding the building pad

- New retaining walls

- Upgraded driveways and/or turn-around

- Backflow preventers

- Upgraded electrical service

- Landscaping upgrades

NOTE: If you had performed any upgrades on your lost house that might be included in Building Code Upgrades (for example double pained windows or additional insulation) they would be included in the general Coverage A since they were a part of the structure prior to the loss.

Landscape Coverage (Trees, Shrubs, Plants and Lawns)

Landscape coverage (sometimes listed as **Trees, Shrubs, Plants and Lawns**) is a separate coverage which usually describes both the removal and replacement of damaged trees. This coverage usually has a per-item or per-tree limit as well as an overall limit. In most cases the overall limit is 5 percent of the Dwelling coverage, and the per-item (or per-tree) limit is $500-$750 for removal *and replacement*.

> The limit for this coverage, including any necessary debris removal, for any one loss event will not exceed 5% of the Coverage A **stated limit**. No more than $750 will be paid for any one tree, shrub or plant. This coverage is additional insurance and is not subject to the Coverage A **stated limit**.
> Except as provided therein, debris removal for trees, shrubs, plants and lawns is not covered under Section I - Extensions of Coverage, **Debris removal**.

Figure 16: Farmers 2007 Renewal Next Generation Policy

To determine how much of this coverage you should claim, you will need a landscape architect or landscaping expert to identify the plants on your property and value their replacement. Have them prepare a written Scope of Work for which you might have to pay.

Other Coverages

The easiest place to find other coverages is to look over the Table of Contents section of your policy. There might be a section labeled "Additional Protection" or "Extensions of Coverage" which will outline other coverages you have. Read over the coverages to make sure you're familiar with them and don't forget to claim them when the time comes.

Specialty coverages might include:

Fire Department Service Charge

If your local fire department charges a fee to service or protect your house.

Identity Fraud

Disaster survivors are more susceptible to Identity Fraud, probably due to their increased handling of their own personal data (i.e. carrying paperwork around, ordering copies of personal paperwork, giving out your personal information to an increased number of people, and the use of frequent temporary addresses).

Take precautions to protect yourself against identity theft.

Power Interruption/Food Spoilage

A loss in power can result in food spoilage, power surge damage to electrical equipment or other damages.

Lock Re-Keying

Once you're done with construction you will most likely want all of your exterior locks to share the same key or even to make sure you have a fresh key that none of the contractors "accidentally" keeps. Insurance will pay for this.

Temporary Repairs After a Loss

Temporary security fencing, barricading broken windows, placement of tarps on roofs are all examples of what might be considered temporary repairs. (See also "Protect Your Property from Further Damage" on page 17.)

Land Stabilization

Some policies offer coverage to stabilize the land after a covered loss. Following a loss, the land may be disturbed during debris, foundation or slab removal and may necessitate compaction and/or other stabilization techniques before the dwelling can be properly repaired or rebuilt. Typically, 5 percent of Coverage A or a limited dollar amount (for example $10,000) is available.

> **Land**
> If a sudden and accidental direct physical loss results in both a covered loss to the **dwelling**, other than the breakage of glass or safety glazing material, and a loss of land stability, **we** will pay up to $10,000 as an additional amount of insurance for repair costs associated with the land. This includes the costs required to replace, rebuild, stabilize or otherwise restore the land necessary to support that part of the **dwelling** sustaining the covered loss.

Figure 17: Land Stabilization Coverage in an Allstate Deluxe HO Policy

Damage Created During Repairs

If something that was previously intact is subsequently damaged during repairs, that new damage should be covered by your insurance company as part of the same claim. California Insurance Code §2695.9 states:

> *When a loss requires repair or replacement of an item or part, any consequential physical damage incurred in making the repair or replacement not otherwise excluded by the policy shall be included in the loss. The insured shall not have to pay for depreciation nor any other cost except for the applicable deductible.*

Should a contractor fail to protect otherwise undamaged hardwood floors, subsequently damaging them with their equipment, the homeowner could claim the cost of repair. In a total loss situation, an example might be previously undamaged driveways and sidewalks destroyed during reconstruction.

Chapter 8 **Negotiating with your Insurance Adjuster**

Tasks For This Chapter

☐ Collect the contact information necessary to "move up the food chain" at your insurance company.

☐ Become familiar with the Insurance Fair Claims Practice Act.

☐ Know your rights regarding a Recorded Statement.

☐ Learn how to write an effective letter. See page 33.

☐ If asked to attend a settlement meeting, organize your documentation (page 96) and consider consulting an attorney prior to the meeting.

If a Lawyer is Already Involved

If you're reading this because a lawyer is already involved in some way, go directly to Chapter 9.

Many things outside of your control can bring a lawyer into the claims process. No matter which party brings a lawyer in first, it is in your best interest to find a reputable "bad faith" or plaintiff's insurance attorney to protect your rights.

If a Lawyer is Already Involved

Recognizing Trouble

Issues Covered by the "Fair Claims Practice Act"

Besides your policy, there are at least two other legal authorities that affect the claim process. One of them is Case Law (See Appendix A for a brief list of cases pertinent to an insurance claim) and the other is State Insurance Law. Both of these can change at any time, and although keeping track of case law is the job for a full time attorney, most states maintain websites offering public access to current insurance law.

For a relatively brief overview of the laws pertaining to insurance claims, see if your state has adopted a version of the **Unfair Claims Settlement Practices Act**. Keep a copy of it and be at least familiar with its content. This section provides you with a condensed version of the rules that govern how a claim is supposed to be handled. It is usually only a few pages long and is fairly readable, particularly when compared to reading legal texts.

Paraphrasing the California code section, these unfair practices include:

- Misrepresenting to claimants any pertinent facts or insurance policy provisions.

- Failing to acknowledge or act reasonably promptly upon communications with respect to claims.

- Failing to affirm or deny coverage of claims in writing within a reasonable time after "Proof of Loss" requirements are completed.

- Failing to act in good faith to effectuate prompt, fair, equitable settlements.

- Forcing insureds to instigate litigation to recover amounts due by offering less than the amounts ultimately recovered.

- Attempting to settle a claim by an insured for less than the amount to which he/she is reasonably entitled by referencing advertising material accompanying an application.

- Attempting to settle a claim on the basis of an application which was altered without notice to the insured.

> *"...see if your state has adopted a version of the 'Unfair Claims Settlement Practices Act'. Keep a copy of it and be at least basically familiar with its content."*

- Failing, after payment of a claim, to inform insureds, upon request by them, of the coverage under which payment was made.

- Telling insureds or claimants that the insurer typically appeals arbitration awards in favor of insureds or claimants for the purpose of compelling them to accept a smaller settlement award or compromise.

- Delaying the investigation or payment of claims by requiring a preliminary claim report and then requiring subsequent submission of formal Proof of Loss forms, both of which contain substantially the same information.

- Failing to settle claims promptly under one portion of the insurance policy coverage in order to influence settlements under other portions of the policy coverage.

- Failing to provide a reasonable explanation based on the facts or applicable law of a denial or offer of a compromise settlement.

- Directly advising a claimant not to obtain the services of an attorney.

- Misleading a claimant as to the applicable statute of limitations.

Recognizing and Dealing with Troublesome Adjusters

Top Dollar Property Claims[24] by Les Watrous includes a great list of the games some adjuster's play to gain the upper hand.

> *[A] troublesome adjuster may either show up too early or too late for a scheduled on-site inspection to catch you 'off guard.' This tactic is sometimes used to make sure your contractor or some other advisor is not in attendance when the adjuster arrives. These troublesome adjusters tend to have overt characteristic traits which may be indicated by the following actions and comments:*

- *Intimidating remarks as to the cause and coverage of your loss*

- *A suspicious attitude about the reason you are filing a loss claim*

- *Being accusatory toward you: "Didn't you help create this situation?"*

- *"Low-Balling" the settlement amount*

- *Delaying the claims process*

- *Not returning calls or inquires*

- *Unethically pressuring you to use his or her contractor to do your repair work*

- *Non-responsive to telephone calls*

- *"Your file is lost"*

- *"I never received your mail"*

- *"I never received your fax"*

- *"Your estimate is miles apart from my evaluation"*

- *"I sent you a letter, didn't you receive it?"*

- *"My supervisor is on vacation"*

- *"I have not been given authority to settle your claim yet"*

- *"I'll be tied up for the next couple of weeks"*

- *"I'll have to request your file from the home office. It might take some time"*

- *Calling you when he/she knows you won't be at home to justify his/her obligation to remain in contact with you ("Well, every time I call the claimant, he's not at home.")*

Recorded Statements

While you have a duty to cooperate with your insurer and a duty to provide a **recorded statement**, not all recorded statements are alike. Often an adjuster will ask for a tape recorded statement at your first meeting, even while you are standing amid your rubble following your loss and in a state of shock. Sometimes the adjuster asks for a tape recorded statement of you, your spouse or relative over the telephone.

If an insurance company representative calls you for a recorded statement over the phone, here are a few tips we have learned from years of listening to people in this same situation:

---

[24] Watrous, Tom. *Top Dollar Property Claims.* TGWB Publishing, 1998.

- If the adjuster insists upon completing a recorded statement, ask the adjuster to simply give you a copy of the questions they are reading and say you will submit written answers to any coverage or agent questions.

- Be firm and polite, but protect yourself from letting your insurance company take advantage of your situation.

- Avoid making recorded statements over the telephone. Politely request that questions be sent to you in writing (email, fax, mail, etc.). You may need to be persistent and ask several times before the questions are finally sent to you.

- You have a duty to your insurance company to describe your LOSS, not your life! You should comfortably answer questions, for instance, related to the quantities, sizes and qualities of your house features and personal property.

- Be cautious but not paranoid. Avoid answering "casual" questions not related to your loss, even if not recorded. The interviewer will be taking notes on your answers. You have no idea in what way your "casual" answer might influence your settlement process.

- We recommend you politely refuse to answer any questions pertaining to the initial purchase of your insurance policy or your policy limits. All the policy information they need should be either in your policy application or obtained by your agent when you got your policy.

- If you have already recorded a statement, send a letter or email to your adjuster requesting that a written transcript and a copy of the audiotape be sent to you within two weeks.

Sample Letter Requesting a Written Transcript

[POLICY NUMBER]

[CLAIM NUMBER]

Dear [**Insurance Company NAME**]:

As you are aware, we lost our home and everything in it during the [**YOUR DISASTER**]. Thank you for everything you have done so far to get us back into our lost home.

Your adjuster made a tape recorded statement of us after our loss on [**DATE**].

Since we were in a state of shock over our loss, we have very limited recollection of what was asked or what was said. We have every intention of cooperating in the adjustment of our loss, but we feel this information will be important for our records.

We respectfully request that you send us a copy of the audio recording that was made and a written transcript of the entire recording immediately.

We expect a response in writing within 15 days.

Thank you for your immediate attention.

Sincerely,

[**Homeowner signature**]

[**Homeowner NAME**]

Delaying Payment

If the insurance company is withholding insurance settlement money from you, you have reason enough to start complaining. Unfortunately, defining what a delay is might be a problem. To an outsider, waiting any length of time for payment might sound unreasonable, but there might be circumstances where a delay could be warranted.

If you have turned in paperwork to justify a payment, don't be afraid to call your adjuster after two weeks and ask where your payment is. If you can't get answers from your adjuster, his manager or the home office, you might consider contacting your Department of Insurance to help solve this problem.

Insurance Company in Direct Contact with Your Contractor

A major point: *Use your own contractor!* A contractor referred by the insurance company might be more interested in pleasing the insurance company than you. You should also know that California Insurance Code §2695.9(b) states: "No insurer shall require that the insured have the property repaired by a specific individual or entity."

Your insurance policy is a contract between you and your insurance company.

> *"Ask your contractor to refrain from talking to the insurance company, and tell your contractor and your adjuster that all questions must go through you."*

Your reconstruction or repair contract is between you and YOUR contractor. The insurance company does not contract with your contractor. Your contractor does not know your insurance policy. Your contractor cannot, by law, negotiate with the insurance company.

If the insurance company tries to negotiate directly with the contractor, it is operating not only against California codes (California Insurance Code §2695.2c and §2695.5), it can greatly complicate your claim. It will put the insurance company between you and YOUR contractor. It will create a barrier between you and YOUR contractor. Remember, the insurance company has a contract with you, NOT your contractor.

If you end up having a problem with your contractor, the insurance company will throw up its hands and tell you the problem is between you and your contractor. They will say they have nothing to do with it, even though their adjuster may have played a role in the issue. (A word of caution: We have had far too many homeowners tell us how much they regret having allowed an adjuster to play a large role in discussions with their contractor.)

For example, your adjuster might start changing actual features or quality choices on the rebuild of your damaged house without your permission, or try to get the contractor to lower prices or cut corners. Payment to the contractor is your responsibility, so you'll want to protect yourself from any situation that could lead to the insurance company reducing its payments to you.

Ask your contractor to refrain from talking to (or negotiating with) the insurance company, and tell your contractor and your adjuster that all questions must go through you. Even if you do not know the answer, you need to maintain control over YOUR construction contract to decide if the question makes a difference in what the insurance company will pay on your claim.

Signs You May Need to Consult an Attorney

Any of the following could be taken as a sign that you need to consult an attorney:

- The insurance company wants you to meet with their lawyer or involves their legal department in your claim process.

- Delaying Payment (depending on circumstance and length of time).

- You are asked to attend a private meeting to "talk things out" –which may mean negotiate a settlement.

- Settlement is offered by the insurance company *before* repairs are complete.

- If the insurance company asks you to sign a waiver or other agreement.

- Language on checks or accompanying paperwork that may limit your claim.

- If you are deposed or asked to "submit to" an EUO (examination under oath) or statement under oath.

- If there is a question as to who caused the loss.

- It has been nine months and you have not come to an agreement with your insurance company or they're being "difficult."

- The insurance company wants you to sign anything beyond a brief statement that a check was received.

- The insurance company refuses to pay you any more money, and you're still not fully compensated for your loss.

"Bad Faith" by Your Insurance Company

In a broad sense, **Bad Faith** is when an insurance company doesn't uphold its duty or acts "unreasonable" with its policyholder. The definition of "unreasonable" is mainly determined by case law so providing a firm definition can prove problematic.[25] "Bad Faith" relates closely to "Unfair Claims Practices."

Most Bad Faith claims stem from:

- Wrongful denial or improper investigation of a claim

- Unreasonable policy interpretation

- Unreasonable settlement offers (within the context of policy limits)

- Lack of willingness to pay a reasonable claim within policy limits

- Unwillingness to defend a lawsuit against a policyholder or to protect a policyholder's assets

Underinsurance is not considered "Bad Faith" but is still a legal issue on which a policyholder's attorney – but not a public adjuster – can investigate and pursue mediation or litigation to resolve.

---

[25] 1/6/11. For examples see:
http://www.bourhis-mann.com/Insurance/How-to-Talk-Back-to-Your-Insurance-Company.htm
or 1/6/11. http://en.wikipedia.org/wiki/Insurance_bad_faith

What You Can Do When You Spot Trouble

Gather Evidence to Prove Your Claim

Before you jump into accusing your adjuster of treating you unfairly, you must first *be prepared*. An insurance claim is basically you providing proof of your monetary damages, but might also include your claim diary and copies of correspondence etc. This workbook's main focus is on gathering this proof. Here are some examples of proof you should have gathered:

- Photographs – digital photos save a lot of time

- Relics and artifacts from your debris

- Written estimate/Scope of Loss for your dwelling and other structures and/or receipts for incurred structural repair expenses

- Complete (as possible) personal property inventory and/or receipts for incurred expenses

- Landscape repair/replace estimate and/or receipts for incurred expenses

- Receipts for incurred Living Expenses

- Estimate of how much your house could have rented for or a lease agreement for your new temporary residence

- Receipts or estimates for any other expenses incurred due to the disaster (see Chapter 6 as a reference)

- A completed Coverage Overview chart (found on page 37). It's impossible to know your bottom line if you don't document it fully

- A list of "unfair" or "bad faith" conduct by your insurance company and its adjusters, if any

- Your claim diary and other documentation of communications (See page 32.)

To Avoid Problems with Adjusters, do the Following:

- Keep a claim diary. See page 11.

- See "Communicating to Protect Your Claim" on page 32.

- Never send originals to the insurance company. Keep copies of everything.

- If an adjuster does not contact you when they told you they would, or if they do not show up for a scheduled appointment, send a *brief* note to the adjuster and the responsible manager to let them know you were inconvenienced.

- If you're having a problem getting in touch with the adjuster, try early in the morning before they get wrapped up in someone else's claim, or even in the late afternoon after they've returned from appointments and are at their desk doing paperwork.

- If you do not agree with something, say so and voice your concern in writing. If you are silent they will assume you agree. We have seen too many homeowners learn too late that their silence was costly and taken as an acceptance of the adjuster's statement.

When You've Done All You Can With Your Current Adjuster

1. Move "up the food chain." Ask to speak to the adjuster's manager. If that doesn't work, talk to that person's supervisor, and move on up the line, if necessary.

2. Join with other survivors.

3. Find a nonprofit/advocacy group for advice.

4. File a complaint with your DOI for non-legal issues (see "Best Use of Your Department of Insurance" below).

5. If you are considering hiring a Public Adjuster, see the section in Chapter 1 on "Public Adjusters" before using this option.

6. Hire a lawyer as a last resort. Avoid THREATENING to use a lawyer against your adjuster or insurance company. See Chapter 9.

Best Use of Your Department of Insurance

If you are experiencing any of the issues listed above, as well as other annoying clerical issues (i.e. lack of communication, not sending the appropriate paperwork or a copy of your policy, etc.) you can contact your **Department of Insurance (DOI)** and file a complaint (Request for Assistance or RFA). Your insurance company will be told there is a complaint and will be asked for an explanation and the DOI will attempt to find a resolution.

There are certain issues that cannot be resolved by your Department of Insurance. The following is from a California Department of Insurance (**CDI**) letter in response to a Request for Assistance:

> "Often disputes of this nature deal with questions of fact or law that the department of insurance may not be empowered to resolve. While this department does not have the legal authority to determine the amount of damages you may recover as a result of your claim or decide matters of legal liability, we understand your concerns and are making every effort to gather information and evaluate the circumstances of your complaint."

One example of "legal liability" is underinsurance. Although the Department of Insurance might like to know about underinsurance so they can gather evidence to try to regulate it in the future (or to levy fines against the company when possible), there is nothing they can legally do for your particular case. If you decide to report a legal issue to them, just be aware of their limitations.

> "If you are experiencing any of the issues listed above, as well as other annoying clerical issues, you can contact the Department of Insurance and file a complaint."

The bottom line is that if you want a resolution to a legal issue, your best bet is to hire a qualified plaintiff's insurance lawyer.

Negotiation Tips

Be aware: insurance companies have attorneys on staff to create their strategies and advise them. Occasionally, we have seen a company send a representative to a negotiation who is educated and trained as an attorney but who hasn't passed the Bar Exam. This allows them to cover themselves while getting around the legal requirement to tell you when an attorney is present so that you have the option of bringing your own attorney. You may meet with these representatives without realizing they are acting in a quasi-legal capacity.

Preparation: Know ALL your numbers and issues.

Patience: Time works in your favor.

Listen: Their words are important but they may not mean what they say.

Understand: You are in control. Your reasonable replacement number is your goal!

Simplify (KISS method – Keep it simple and short.) Convey your message in as few words as possible.

Persistence: Don't give up. Concede a point when you are satisfied it is fair.

Useful tips:

- Do not hurry – it leads to confusion and mistakes.

- There can be more than one meeting – it is your choice.

- Unless you are fully prepared, the initial meeting should be short. If you are not prepared, a long initial meeting works in their favor because the insurance company will have a better chance to "size you up" and learn the weaknesses of your case.

- If you find that you are not prepared, get out quickly and keep your strengths for another day.

- You always have the power to walk out. "I need to go now and come back later" can be a sign of strength.

- Take any release home to think about it.

- It is not the end; unless you sign a release, there can always be another meeting.

- Clarify all terms and numbers. "I got lost here. Please explain," is an OK response.

- Separate "old" money from "new" money. "Old" money is money already paid or can be the remaining unpaid policy limits. "New" money is additional money beyond what had previously been considered for payment.

- Know your weaknesses.

- Know your strengths.

- Be flexible and fair – but do not surrender.

- Keep as much "on the table" as possible. Once you concede something to the insurance company, it's practically impossible to put that item back on the table to renegotiate.

- Negotiate with the adjuster, not with yourself. Save any compromises for the bargaining table.

Chapter 9 **Hiring Professionals to Help with Your Claim**

Tasks for This Chapter

☐ Know what questions to ask the professional while interviewing them for the job.

☐ Research qualified plaintiff's attorneys. Don't reject an attorney just because they are out of your immediate area. You want the best, not the closest.

☐ Review any contract before signing.

Professionals Available to Help With Your Claim

Public Adjuster

Do not confuse the insurance adjuster or independent (insurance) adjuster with a **public adjuster**. The Public Adjuster is a professional licensed by your state to work on your behalf for a fee. The Public Adjuster receives a percentage of your insurance settlement. Please use extreme caution when considering a public adjuster and read the section titled "Public Adjusters," Chapter 2 page 19.

Contractor

A **construction contractor** is a licensed professional whom you can hire to create a Scope of Loss, or repair or rebuild your house. It is beyond the scope of this book to discuss all of the details involved in hiring a contractor when repairing or rebuilding your home, but if hiring a specialized contractor for a Scope of Loss, here are some things to keep in mind:

- Do they have experience testifying in court?

- Do they have experience defending their scope to the insurance company outside of court?

- Do they actually build houses for a living?

- Ask for references. The references should include homeowners and attorneys. A contractor who creates a defendable Scope of Loss will have happy homeowners for clients and a good relationship with attorneys who defend homeowners.

- NOTE: The above may seem nonsensical as you begin your insurance negotiations, but be aware that you'll want to be just as prepared as your insurance company undoubtedly will be. In the background, your adjuster or his/her supervisor is already considering the same issues. Every loss, to them, could eventually lead to some form of mediation or legal action.

A detailed Scope of Loss takes time and will cost money. Most people tell us that it was the best money they spent. Beware of the following when signing a contract for a Scope of Loss:

- Monetary limits: Make sure you're not signing an open-ended contract on how much you'll be spending. Ask for a flat rate. Some contractors charge a fee of $1 or $1.50 per square foot of your lost house, but make sure your bottom line is agreed upon in advance.

- Deadlines: Make sure a deadline for completion is specified in the contract.

- Define the final product: What will the contractor deliver to you for the money you're paying?

- Define additional services: What services are offered beyond the actual scope and what are the costs associated with them? For example, how much will they charge if they have to meet with the insurance company to explain the scope? Define it now so you're not surprised later.

Real Estate Agent

A **real estate agent** might be used for finding a rental, a comparable rental quote, selling your lot or buying a replacement home. When interviewing a real estate agent, here are some questions to ask:

- What experience do you have in my neighborhood?

- Do you do this full time?

- Do you personally handle negotiations?

- How long have you been in real estate and what is your track record? When was your last transaction? *The number of years they've held a license is not equal to number of transactions.*

- Ask for references and then follow up by contacting the references.

What you should consider before signing a contract with a real estate agent:

- Be aware of long-term contracts: make sure there is an "out" if this agent doesn't perform well.

Attorneys and the Insurance Claim

During the insurance claim process, a **lawyer** might be needed to review paperwork presented to you by the insurance company, to negotiate with your insurance company if your settlement comes to a standstill, or to protect your rights if the insurance company has acted so terribly you believe you have a legal case against them (see page 95).

Talking about attorneys can be scary for some people as they don't want to "go that far" or push their insurance company too hard. But in order to fully understand your rights, it's a good idea to research this option. Even if you decide against litigation, give yourself enough time to make an informed decision. Give yourself at least that peace of mind.

> *"...in order to fully understand your rights, it's a good idea to research [hiring an attorney]."*

Almost all California fire and homeowner insurance policies contain a provision that limits the time to file a lawsuit to one year following the date of the loss (see page 35). If you believe your insurance company underinsured you or treated you unfairly, improperly, or in "bad faith," you will need to review your circumstances with a qualified plaintiff's insurance attorney to see if you need to comply with the one-year deadline. The area in which a plaintiff's attorney specializes can make a big difference. One who specializes in insurance law is the most qualified person to assess any benefits and remedies you may have under your insurance policy and the law.

Do not wait until the last few weeks or days before the one-year deadline! Attorneys will be busy with other disaster survivors and less available to handle your evaluation. It takes time to adequately review your situation and prepare paperwork.

Be aware that some insurance companies may drag their feet in some clever ways in an effort to let the one-year deadline in your policy expire. Be aware and do not let this happen. Understand all your options long before the deadline expires.

Before Resorting to Litigation

- Make your best efforts to reasonably obtain all of your policy limits.

- If that's not possible, write your adjuster(s) and get paid for any outstanding "undisputed" amounts. The "undisputed" amount is the amount that you both agree is *at least* the amount the insurance company owed. For example, if the insurance company thinks they owe you $15,000 to finish your ALE and you think they owe you $25,000, then the amount that both your adjuster and you agree the insurance company owes you is $15,000. The $15,000 is "undisputed." The difference, or the "disputed" amount, is $10,000.

  Don't be afraid to accept the "undisputed" amount. That money makes a bigger difference in your bank account than it does sitting in theirs.

- Gather your documentation. See the section in Chapter 8 titled "Gather Evidence to Prove Your Claim" on page 96.

- Send a Request for Assistance (RFA) to the Department of Insurance (CDI) informing them of any insurance process issues. See "Best Use of Your Department of Insurance" on page 97.

- Send a certified letter along with your completed Scope of Loss to your insurance company requesting full payment of your claim within 15 days or, if they will not, to provide in writing all reasons why they will not.

- Consult with a qualified plaintiff's insurance attorney.

You owe it to yourself to have your insurance recovery evaluated by a qualified legal professional and learn all of your options before the end of the one-year policy deadline for legal action. Be fully informed before signing any insurance settlement release or making a final decision!

What You Should Consider When Selecting an Attorney

The following tips should be considered when selecting an attorney:

> *TIP: Fees are negotiable even after an attorney fee agreement has been signed.*

- Always use an appropriate specialist. Would you go to a plumber if you had an electrical problem? Do not go to any attorney other than an insurance law attorney for any reason associated with an insurance claim. An insurance settlement situation or a contract that looks "reasonable" to one attorney might prove unreasonable to an attorney knowledgeable with insurance law.

- If an attorney makes a verbal promise, make sure they put that commitment in writing – preferably in the contract.

- When hiring an attorney to take on a complicated case such as insurance bad faith or underinsurance, do not hire the attorney on an hourly basis. For simple matters such as a brief review of insurance correspondence, an hourly fee makes sense. However, if the simple matter moves into more complicated issues, consider switching your contract to a "contingency fee" arrangement.

- A contingency agreement is a contract in which the attorney agrees to represent you without any upfront costs, in return for a percentage of your settlement or award amount. If there is no monetary award or settlement, then they receive only their costs. See below for more information about contingency agreements.

- Do not expect frequent communication from a contingency attorney. Unlike an hourly fee attorney who may be billing you by the minute for email correspondence and phone calls, a lawyer working on contingency generally will not call you unless they need information from you.

- Avoid taking offense at an attorney's gruffness or seemingly rude manner. What is important is their track record in negotiating with the insurance company.

- Put reputation, competence and track record above their proximity to you. Sometimes the best attorney doesn't work in your town. Having the best attorney is more important than having an attorney with an office right around the corner.

What You Should Know About Contingency Agreements

An attorney contingency fee agreement is a contract in which the attorney receives as payment a percentage of your settlement or award. The attorney does not get paid if he/she loses your case. Some agreements can be very confusing. Read the fee agreement carefully as it may have hidden costs. Be cautious.

- The first thing you should know is that contingency agreements are negotiable; fees are not set in stone by law, statute or by case law.

- The agreement will include the specific legal costs of *your* case and the fee. The **costs** include expert fees (preparation, travel, lodging and testimony), valuation experts, exhibits, messengers, photocopying, court reporters, court and filing fees, and more. Legal costs and expenses must be *directly related* to your case and should be spent wisely and effectively. Expenses in any lawsuit, even shared or pro-rated with other plaintiffs, can be considerable. The fee is the percentage that the attorney, including his/her staff and law firm, earn and do not include the specific legal costs of your case.

- Because of the significant cost of an actual trial, some lawyers may not be willing to negotiate that part of the fee (usually 40 percent), but there are other parts of the agreement they might be willing to negotiate. For example, they might be willing to charge only 20 percent if the case is settled before court papers are filed or 30 percent if the case settles before trial and 40 percent if it goes to trial.

- Most contracts specify that you pay for costs or expenses on top of the fee. Make sure you get any verbal agreements about expenses in writing. Do not make any assumptions or take the attorney's word for it. You should be clear up front about any expenses for which you will be responsible.

- Ask about, and do not accept, high costs such as $2-a-page photocopies, first-class travel or 5-star hotel rooms. Ask to see a fee schedule ahead of time. You will want to be aware of these charges and negotiate those types of costs. You may even specify that travel be done in economy class instead of first class. Negotiation before signing a contract can save you money.

- What happens if you lose? Unless your contingency fee agreement clearly states you will *not* be charged for costs if you lose your case, your attorney can still charge you those expenses. Some law firms with substantial resources do *not* charge for costs if you lose your case or have no recovery. Still, a plaintiff could lose his/her case and still owe substantial costs.

- What is the scope of obligation under this agreement? Does it end after trial? What happens if the case is sent to appeal?

- You will also want to be sure you understand *when* expenses are to be paid. For example, some firms want expenses paid monthly while others are willing to wait until the settlement or award is complete.

- Once you sign an agreement, the attorney can place a lien on your settlement to collect their fees and costs.

CAUTION: Be careful to check if the attorney fees are based on **GROSS** instead of **NET** of your settlement money.

- Fees based on GROSS will always cost you more in attorney fees.

- GROSS means you are also paying attorney fees on the costs the attorney decides to incur on your case. (Besides filing, expert and witness fees, and photocopying, this could include travel and lodging costs.)

- GROSS means the attorney has no incentive to keep costs down. The attorney gets a percentage on every dollar spent. The more he/she spends, the more you pay in actual attorney fees.

- Fees on NET mean YOU GET MORE money! See EXAMPLE below.

EXAMPLE: You are awarded $500,000. COSTS of litigation are $100,000.	
Fees based on GROSS	**Gross award $500,000**
You pay 40% attorney fee before paying COSTS	- 200,000
You pay costs	- 100,000
YOU end up with	**$200,000**

Fees based on NET	**Gross award $500,000**
You pay COSTS first	- 100,000
Net Award	**400,000**
You pay 40% in attorney fees after paying COSTS	-160,000
YOU end up with	**$240,000**

CAUTION: Be careful of attorneys who ask for "up front" money in exchange for a fee percentage reduction.

- Asking you for money to litigate your claim could mean the attorney is under-funded or does not have enough confidence in winning your case to use his/her money for your costs.

- Be sure the law firm has the money and qualified staff to finance and withstand multi-million dollar complex litigation.

- An under-funded attorney can give up a lot of your money during a settlement negotiation to get a quick settlement.

- Expert costs can be very high in complex "valuation" cases (which many insurance cases are). Even extensive mediation can require experts and prove costly.

CAUTION: If the attorney says he will reduce his percentage but then gives you a long attorney fee agreement with confusing clauses, this could actually inflate your final legal expenses. Attorney fee agreements should be concise and easy to understand.

In summary, be sure to:

1. Review and understand any attorney fee agreement before signing it.

2. Check that fees are based on **NET** not **GROSS** fees on your award money.

3. Check online:

   - Does your attorney and law firm appear to have sufficient resources to fund a complex and costly case?

   - Does your attorney have the appropriate background and experience to go against your insurance company?

   - What kind of specialization and experience does the law firm have?

For More Information on Using an Attorney During Your Claim

- *How to Make Insurance Companies Pay Your Claims*, by William Shernoff, (Hastings House, 1990). Refer to a 10-page section beginning on Page 73. It is highly recommended.

- *Claim Paid: A Consumer's Guide Through the Insurance Claims Maze*, by Frank Dumas (Stratton Pr, 1990), includes an excellent information about hiring an attorney in chapter 8.

How to Find the Best Professional for You

Ask members of your community, a lawyer you already know (maybe your family attorney) or the bar association for attorneys who specialize in insurance law. After a disaster, you might run into professionals at community meetings. Do not sign an agreement on site. If you think you will need their services you should set up a time to have a private consultation.

Any professional worth their salt should want to have a consultation with you and should not charge for this preliminary meeting. Bring any and all paperwork (remember the file container and diary?) to this meeting to be sure they have access to all of the information they may need.

- Make a brief timeline and outline pertinent to your specific situation.

- Be concise and to the point. Do not waste your time or theirs.

- Avoid details of the loss event unless describing "how you escaped the tornado" applies to the expertise of the professional you are hiring.

Take this opportunity to find out if the professional is right for you. Make a list of questions beforehand so you remember to ask them during the interview.

Find a professional with extensive related experience, with appropriately documented and professionally presented cases or projects, and with the financial and business resources to follow your project or case to the end.

"Find a professional with extensive related experience, with appropriately documented and professionally presented cases or projects, and with the financial and business resources to follow your project or case to the end."

Can I Fire a Professional After I Hired Them?

An attorney, a public adjuster or most other professionals, can be terminated by you at any time, as long as you do so in writing. Be aware that if you do cancel the fee agreement or hourly contract, you owe the "reasonable value" of the services performed to date on your behalf.

Even though many states provide that you can cancel a Public Adjuster contract within 72 hours, most states allow you to terminate a public adjuster at any time, with or without cause even after the 72-hour cancellation deadline. Your state may differ, so consult with an attorney before cancellation.

In Closing

We are sorry and saddened that you had your loss but it is why we are here. We hope that you will come to a successful resolution of your claim and that the results are as close to "break even" in your hypothetical poker game as possible.

Every claim is different and insurance claim tactics change constantly. Suggestions and recovery experiences from disaster survivors are greatly appreciated and are always welcome. Please feel free to contact us using the "Contact Us" section of our website www.carehelp.org. There you will also find up-to-date recovery information and claim tips. Register, too, for our free newsletter.

Appendix A – Important California Case Law

Brandt v. Superior Court - 37 Cal3d 813 (1985)

When an insurer tortiously withholds benefits, attorney's fees, reasonably incurred to compel payment of the policy benefits, are recoverable as an element of the damages resulting from such tortious conduct.

Prudential-LMI v. Superior Court 51 Cal.3d 674 , 692-93 (1990)

The state's one-year limitation period on suits is subject to equitable tolling from the time that an insured gives notice of a claim until the time that the insured is formally notified in writing that coverage will be denied.

Free v. Republic - 8 CA4 1726 (1992)

In answering an insured's question about how much insurance to buy, an insurance agent owed a duty of reasonable care to the insured.

Conway v. Farmers Home Mutual - 26 Cal. App. 4th 1185 (1994)

An insured homeowner may recover the replacement cost of fire damage to an insured home by purchasing another home at another location.

Desai v. Farmers - 47 CA4 1011 (1996)

A "value protection" clause in a property insurance policy created an ambiguity that could lead the reasonable insured to believe that s/he was covered in excess of the stated policy limit.

An insurer may be vicariously liable for its agent's negligence in failing to obtain the coverage requested by an insured or to sufficiently inform the insured of the coverage that was obtained.

An insurer owes its insured a fiduciary duty to act in the utmost good faith.

Paper Savers v. Nasca - 51 CA4 1090 (1997)

An agent who makes representations regarding the effect of coverage purchased by an insured owes the insured a duty of reasonable care in making those representations.

Rattan v. USAA - 84 CA4 715 (2000)

When an insurance carrier recommends and guarantees the work of a general contractor in repairing insured property, the contractor's failure to perform adequately is not sufficient to support a tort claim, including a claim for bad faith, against the insurer.

Fire Insurance Exchange v. Superior Court - Cal. App. LEXIS 251 (2004)

A reasonable insured would expect the replacement cost provision to provide coverage for increased building code costs if necessary.

E.M.M.I. Inc. v. Zurich Am. Ins. Co., 32 Cal. 4th 465, 470-71 (2004)

If a provision has no "clear and explicit meaning," ambiguity is "resolved by interpreting the ambiguous provisions in the sense the insurer believed the insured understood them at the time of formation.

Everett v. State Farm - 162 Cal.App.4th 649 (Cal. Ct. App. 2008)

Insureds cannot pursue contract or tort remedies where [*the insured never questioned their coverage, asked for a policy review or a site visit*] (1) the policy language clearly limits coverage to the stated limits and the insurance company paid all that was owed, (2) the policy unambiguously states that it is the insured's responsibility to maintain adequate insurance, and (3) there is no evidence that the agent who sold the policy made any misrepresentations.

Glossary

actual cash value: (ACV) The amount your insurance company will pay you for damage to covered property after the insurance company deducts an arbitrary amount of depreciation

ACV: See *Actual Cash Value*

additional living expenses: (ALE) Living expenses incurred by a homeowner or family above and beyond his or its normal expenses due to a covered loss. Also referred to as Loss of Use.

adjuster: A negotiator of an insurance claim who determines the amount of the loss the insurer is willing to pay.

  insurance adjuster: Any adjuster hired by the insurance company to represent it.

  outside adjuster: An insurance adjuster who is not an employee of the insurance company.

  public adjuster: A licensed professional a policyholder may choose to hire to represent him/her against the insurance company.

adjusting (or, "to adjust"): The give and take process of negotiating an insurance claim.

agent: The sales person who sells insurance policies.

ALE: See *Additional Living Expenses*

as built: Usually referring to the description or drawings of a structure as it stands, or stood prior to a loss.

assessment: See *Home Owner Association Assessment*

attorney: A licensed professional hired to represent an entity's interest in matters of law and/or insurance interpretations, rights and benefits. Used interchangeably with Lawyer.

bad faith: When an insurance company doesn't uphold its duty or acts unreasonable with its policyholder.

break-even: To have been monetarily compensated equal to what was lost or damaged.

building code upgrade: Insurance coverage applied when the local or state governments impose new building standards.

California Department of Insurance: (CDI or DOI) "The California Department of Insurance is responsible for enforcing many of the insurance-related laws of the state" tasked "to protect insurance consumers by regulating the industry's practices."

case law: Previous court cases that are referred to by an attorney or the courts when arguing or making a judicial decision on a legal matter.

CDI: See *California Department of Insurance*

claim: See *Insurance Claim*

claimant: The person or entity that files the insurance claim.

contents: See *Personal Property*

contingency agreement: A contract in which the attorney agrees to represent you without any upfront costs, in return for a percentage of your settlement or award amount actually won.

coverage: The insurance protection afforded to you by the policy.

covered loss: Damage to insured property that will be paid by the insurance company.

debris removal coverage: Insurance funds available to remove destroyed real and personal property from the premises.

dec page: See *Declaration Page*

declaration page: An overview of policy information, including the name and address of the insured and property, the dollar and/or percentage amounts of coverages, the deductible amount, the name(s) of the mortgagee(s) and ALL applicable endorsement forms. Also referred to as a Dec Page.

deductible: The monetary portion of the loss which you are to pay and clearly written on the Dec Page

department of insurance: (DOI or, in California, CDI) The state agency responsible for enforcing and regulating the insurance-related laws of the state.

depreciation: The loss in value from all causes, including age, and wear and tear.

    excessive depreciation: When the insurance company depreciates more than is reasonable.

DOI: See *Department of Insurance*

dwelling coverage: The primary coverage of any homeowner policy that covers the main living or rental structure on the property.

endorsements: Additional policy forms stated on the Declaration Page(s) that change the policy conditions and can increase or decrease coverages in the policy.

evidence: The documentation you create to justify your claim.

extended replacement: An extra amount of money available to a policyholder that is above and beyond the stated dwelling limit of the policy.

Fair Claims Practice Act: A summary of the state consumer regulatory laws pertaining to insurance claims.

forbearance: A "lending mercy" where the payment terms of your loan are temporarily changed to your benefit by the mortgage holder.

general conditions: Expense items which are necessary for the repair of damages or reconstruction of a house but which are not the direct costs of materials and labor to rebuild the house such as water, electricity, emergency and security fencing, and a port-a-potty. Also referred to as Soft costs.

HOA: See *Home Owner Association*

hold back: The amount of money withheld by the insurance company for depreciation.

home owner association: (HOA) A legal entity consisting of homeowners living within a defined boundary, tasked to care for common areas and to create visual consistency within that boundary.

home owner association assessment: A fee charged to the homeowners within the HOA to pay for damages or improvements to the common areas.

insurance claim: An assertion by a homeowner that an insurance company should pay for insured damages to their property following a covered loss.

land stabilization: Insurance funds available in some policies for limited expenses to stabilize the land supporting the structure after a covered loss.

landscape coverage: Additional insurance available for plants, vegetation and landscape features such as sprinklers.

lawyer: See *Attorney*

lien: A legal claim filed against a property held as security until a debt is paid.

like kind and quality: A standard applied for the replacement product or building material (or even living arrangements) equal to what you had prior to your loss.

line of sight: A standard applied to the extent of reasonably uniform repair to all surfaces and elements that you can clearly see in your line of sight while observing the damaged or destroyed area.

litigation: The legal process when one entity sues another entity to settle a dispute.

loss: Damage to property without regard to coverage. *See also Covered Loss.*

loss of use: See *Additional Living Expenses*

mitigate damages: A duty a policyholder has to take every reasonable step to make sure that more damage does not occur to the damaged or destroyed property.

negotiation: The give and take process of coming to a final agreement. Insurance adjusting requires negotiation by the adjuster and the claimant.

other structures coverage: Insurance funds available for permanent structures on the property that are not part of the dwelling.

payoff letter: A letter generated by the mortgage company stating the exact dollar amount needed to satisfy full payment of the mortgage.

personal property: The tangible items on your real property that are not attached to the buildings or land. *Also referred to as Contents*

> **personal property coverage**: Insurance funds available for personal property contents.

> **personal property inventory**: The detailed documentation created by a claimant to substantiate the replacement cost of the damaged or destroyed personal property.

> **personal property list**: See *Personal property Inventory*

policy: The legal contract purchased by a policy holder from the insurance company.

policy limits: The monetary limits associated with your insurance coverages and stated on your declaration page.

premium: The money paid by the homeowner for the policy.

proof of Loss: A legal document sworn before a notary that declares your total insured loss.

public adjuster: See *Adjuster, Public Adjuster*

RCV: See *Replacement Cost Value*

recorded statement: A record of answers, usually on tape or in a letter, by the policy holder to insured loss related questions provided by the insurance company.

recovery: When you feel you are finally finished with the day to day tasks associated with "fixing" the results of the disaster OR when you have moved on.

release (as in, "sign a release"): A binding FINAL agreement in a document signed by one entity that releases liability of the other party. A FULL release means any dispute is OVER.

repair/rebuild estimate: A detailed estimate of costs to repair damage or rebuild a structure.

replacement cost value: (RCV) The full cost, including today's full retail price with sales tax and delivery, of replacing an item.

request for assistance: (RFA) An official request to the DOI for help in resolving an issue with your insurance company or its adjuster.

RFA: See *Request for Assistance*

settlement: A monetary amount agreed upon by both parties to close a claim.

scope of loss: A detailed itemization of the quantity and quality of every construction component, including all labor, material and soft costs, to replicate your damaged or destroyed home and, when necessary, other structures.

soft costs: *See General Conditions*

underinsured: A predicament you find yourself in after a large or total property loss when you add up the costs of your damaged and destroyed property and your insurance coverages are not enough to pay for replacing or repairing your lost property.

undisputed amount: The amount the insurance company and you have agreed is the least amount owed you for your insured loss. Any additional costs or monies are your "disputed" loss.

About CARe, Inc.

CARe is an educational 501(c)3 nonprofit California corporation established by San Fernando Valley community leaders after the 1994 Northridge earthquake.

Our mission is to provide free comprehensive information about disaster recovery, including the insurance claim process, to disaster survivors so they may effectively re-establish their homes, lives and communities.

Navigating the maze of disaster recovery is an overwhelming task to many survivors. We ease the burden by educating people so they can navigate more effectively through the process.

All CARe volunteers and staff have lost their homes and successfully recovered from disasters. It is the passion for "paying it forward" that draws survivors back to our organization to help survivors of the next disaster.

CARe devoted its first seven years to helping survivors of the Northridge earthquake navigate the often difficult road to recovery. Due to the overwhelming number of claims resulting from the earthquake, we honed our knowledge of the insurance claim process. Since that time, CARe has helped tens of thousands of survivors devastated by a range of natural disasters: from hurricanes in the Southeast and tornadoes in the Midwest, to Southwest wildfires and California firestorms. As a result of our work after the 2007 Southern California wildfires, more than $40 million above policy limits were reclaimed from insurers for the residents of fire-devastated communities.

Many have found the emotional support CARe offers to be an invaluable part of their recovery. But CARe is also focused on results: CARe's volunteer work has brought over $3 billion in economic recoveries to disaster devastated communities across the United States since 1995.

About the Authors

George Kehrer is a fire survivor. He lost his home and two businesses in the Oakland, California firestorm in 1991. Since that disaster, he has worked extensively with thousands of firestorm, hurricane, tornado and earthquake victims. By profession, he is a California licensed attorney and a retired general contractor. He has provided thousands of volunteer hours of research, inspections, testimony and instruction in disaster recovery issues.

Lila Hayes's mother's house, the home Lila grew up in, was destroyed in the 2003 Southern California wildfires. Assuming the tasks of recovery for her mother, Lila struggled through the challenges of survivor recovery. Her focus and energy led her to CARe survivor recovery meetings at a local church. Through these meetings, she started the ad hoc organization, the Old Fire Recovery Group, to help fire survivors in San Bernardino. Through Lila's complete immersion in the recovery process, Lila's mother was able to return to a new house that more fully meets the needs of the 21st century. Following Hurricane Katrina, she advised survivors in association with the Los Angeles non-profit group, Community Partners. She now serves on the Board of Directors for CARe, maintains their website, and advises survivors of other disasters.

Made in the USA
San Bernardino, CA
30 July 2013